HIDDEN TWINS

Other titles in the UKCP Series:

HIDDEN TWINS

What Adult Opposite Sex Twins Have to Teach Us

Olivia Lousada

On behalf of the United Kingdom Council
for Psychotherapy

KARNAC

First published in 2009 by
Karnac Books Ltd
118 Finchley Road, London NW3 5HT

British Library Cataloguing in Publication Data

A C.I.P. for this book is available from the British Library

ISBN-13: 978 1 85575 741 7

Edited, designed and produced by The Studio Publishing Services Ltd,
www.publishingservicesuk.co.uk
e-mail: studio@publishingservicesuk.co.uk

Printed in Great Britain

www.karnacbooks.com

CONTENTS

LIST OF ILLUSTRATIONS

ACKNOWLEDGEMENTS

I would like to thank so many of my family, friends, and colleagues who have supported me in this endeavour. Those I would especially like to thank are here listed in the place in which they entered this story, but are also grouped in the roles that they have played: Earliest and most central of all, my twin brother, Julian, without whom I would never have started this project.

The opposite sex twins who were the co-researchers.

Audrey Sandbank's encouragement to get started.

Dr Sue Jennings in helping me make the first steps in the research.

Dr Kate Maguire for her many hours of consultation, encouragement, and belief in the research and the book.

Steve Moles for the making and editing of the film.

Dr Paula Reardon for reading the text of the book in its early form and her continued support, friendship, and capacity to struggle with minutiae.

Dr John Casson for his enthusiasm for the subject and for some of my writing, and my interpretation of *Twelfth Night* as a consequence of this work.

Dr Alida Gersie for her constant support for rigour on the long and lonely road that always has another horizon to go.

Dr Edward Schiefflin for his academic experience and capacity to repeatedly tell the story of what I have been doing in a different way.

Sandra Lousada for the very many hours she has contributed to the photographic layout for the research and the book.

Erica Hunningher, Kerry Lane and Farquhar McKay for their editorial support.

Leo Lapworth for his wizardry on the web.

Laurie Lapworth for his designs for the web, flyer, and posters for the research.

Case Roos for hours of computer support and lengthy discussions.

Carmel Lousada-Stiven in her enthusiasm for me to complete the task.

My mother, for her creative rigour and humility as political endeavour.

My father, for his capacity to see the exquisite.

Olivia Lousada works as a psychodramatist and psychotherapist in mental health settings. She has a particular focus on the resolution of long-standing difficulties related to family dynamics. She also sculpts and dances. Her professional interests are underpinned by previous training as a Montessori teacher and social worker. Her doctorate studies, on which this book is built, focused on the inter- and intra-personal worlds of opposite sex twins. She is interested in this topic because she is one herself.

Dedicated to
Kate Maguire

PREFACE

If we have met opposite sex twins we have not realized it (Joan).

During the course of the research and book I am delighted to say that I have come across or heard about opposite sex twins who are at peace with their twinship. It is a part of their relationship experience and not a hidden component. This book illuminates adult opposite sex twinship that has been undervalued and even hidden. In so doing, it contributes to the changing attitudes towards the roles of siblings, twins, multiples, and opposite sex twins.

It is when we do this foolish, time-consuming, romantic, quixotic, childlike thing called play that we are most practical, most useful, and most firmly grounded in reality, because the world itself is the most unlikely of places, and it works in the oddest of ways, and we wonít make any sense of it by doing what everybody else has done before us.
It is when we fool about with the stuff the world is made of that we make the most valuable discoveries, we create the most lasting beauty, we discover the most profound truths. The youngest children can do it, and the greatest artist and greatest scientists do it all the time.

(Pullman, *The Guardian*, 22.1.2005)

Introduction

CAPTAIN: When you . . .
Hung on our driving boat, I saw your brother
Most provident in peril, bind himself,—
Courage and hope both teaching him the practice,—
To a strong mast that liv'd upon the sea;
Where, like Arion on the dolphin's back,
I saw him hold acquaintance with the waves
So long as I could see.
VIOLA: For saying so there's gold.

(Shakespeare, *Twelfth Night*, 1601, 1.11: 9–15)

Let me alert you to the beginning of the story from which this book grew. It was never part of my grand design, either professionally or as an opposite sex twin, to get drawn into the subject of opposite sex twins, into research, and into writing a book, but when it fell upon my path, I woke up to the realization that the task could be mine. There was no going back. My apprehension, I discovered, is frequent among opposite sex twins, but I, like Viola, a female opposite sex twin in Shakespeare's *Twelfth Night*, was churlish enough to be dragged into the story. Viola, disguised as her twin, is set up to fight a man she hears is *a tiger of a knight*, but who is in truth the timid Sir Andrew Aguecheek, who prefers to dance. What complications! I knew this research would be difficult but I had no idea that to illuminate a hidden subject or taboo would meet with such complexity and so much resistance in others and in me. This was neatly expressed by Nancy Segal (1999) who called opposite sex twins the "unseen twins" because they are neither the same sex nor identical in appearance and are, therefore, often unobserved. Think about it. How often do you recognize them when they are together in the street? Hence, I hope to help people to recognize opposite sex twins more readily and to better understand them.

The task of raising opposite sex twins is, in many ways, similar to other twins and siblings. However, as with all sibling positions, be they only children, eldest, middle, youngest, or same sex twins, they each have their own peculiarities unique to their sibling role. With this in mind, the peculiarities unique to opposite sex twins need to be understood by parents and carers of twins as well as by opposite sex twins themselves. Their unique experiences have a complex relationship with our culture and with contemporary psychotherapy theory, in which relationships are seen to be rooted in pairs. The pairing starts with a man and woman, which can lead to conception followed by the relationship pair of mother and baby. During the past century, the mother–baby relationship has been seen to be imperative for mental health because it is at the fulcrum of the psyche. The development of triangular relationships, called the Oedipal conflict, then follows. The importance of pairing has also been endorsed by the fascinating and growing neuro-biological field, in which physical touch is now understood to be central to the development of the brain and psyche. This is marvellous, but problematic for twins. The first relationship for twins is not a unique and exclusive one with mother. The expected condition of humans is to be unique. This is challenged by twins. Neuro-biological research on opposite sex twins is awaited.

My research took place with the participation of three pairs of adult opposite sex twins. The book is not definitive; it reflects the shared experiences of this particular group of adult opposite sex twins. The outcome emerges from a tapestry of different relational threads woven together from activities, painting, and reflection that expressed the expectations, confusions, and surprises of these opposite sex twins. The research makes a contribution to both the growing awareness of relationship experiences of opposite sex twins and to the current discourses in psychotherapy theory and practice. It could be a basis for further research on opposite sex twins, as well as comparative studies between twins and singletons.

The readership for this book is various. It is written for those with interests in:

- the relationship experience of opposite sex twins for personal reasons;
- the relationship experience of opposite sex twins for professional reasons;
- the philosophy of spontaneity, sociometric practice, and research.

If this book is read sequentially the gaze moves from one aspect to another, like watching twins. However, depending on the interests of the reader, there are different pathways through the book:

The academic stories	Chapter One	The existing knowledge
	Chapter Nine	The archive of the findings
The family stories	Chapter Two	The pen pictures of the oppo site sex twins and my roles
	Chapter Seven	The stories of their families
	Chapter Eight	The opposite sex twins similarity to, and difference from, siblings and same sex twins
The research stories	Chapter Three	The philosophy of spontaneity
	Chapter Four	The research design
	Chapter Five	Workshop 1 Comments by the opposite sex twins during Workshop 1
	Chapter Six	Workshop 2 The opposite sex twins' reflections on Workshop 1 and the individual interviews

For the research methodology, see www.hiddentwins.com

CHAPTER ONE

What is the existing knowledge on opposite sex twins?

> VIOLA: My brother he is in Elysium.
> Perchance he is not drown'd. What say you sailors?
> CAPTAIN: It is perchance that you yourself were sav'd.
>
> (Shakespeare, *Twelfth Night*, 1601, 1.11: 4–6)

The subject of this chapter poses a very important question, but, when I started my research, I postponed reading a wide range of literature as I did not want to second guess or interpret my research material with other people's ideas in my head. This was congruent with my practice of psychodrama. Moreno, the inventor of psychodrama, held that we should meet and encounter people, as far as possible, without preconceptions.

However, as an opposite sex twin, I was also scared of what I would find out. Therefore, I undertook a small preliminary enquiry. The research of Klaning, Bo Mortensen and Ohm Kyvik (1996) suggested that the mental health of opposite sex twins was more at risk than that of singletons and same sex twins. This, along with the poignant observations on opposite sex twins made by Audrey Sandbank in conversation, gave me the courage to take up research.

1

In 2001, I attended the Congress for the International Society for Twin Studies. Here, I discovered that there are many growing organizations across the world promoting awareness of twins through research and support for their families. In the UK, St Thomas's Hospital, London, researches twins for what they can teach us about human genetic disposition such as food preference, belief in God, mysticism, divorce, exercise, and the effects of social class, to name but a few. There are also organizations in the UK with international reputations: The Twins and Multiple Births Association and The Multiple Birth Foundation UK. These and other organizations (see Appendix I) reflect the concern for twins, multiple birth siblings, and their families. They recognize the need not only for ongoing research that can contribute to science, education, and psychotherapy, but research that can contribute to the welfare and healthy development of twins. I returned to a more in-depth review of the literature once I had carried out, filmed, and transcribed the activities from my research. These activities influenced which aspects of the literature I looked into more closely. The selected aspects of my literature review in turn gives a picture of some of the developing consciousness of knowledge in the twin field to which this research belongs.

The public debate

During the past seven years of this research, the media has reported the tragic case of a separated-in-infancy opposite sex twin pair who, unaware of their blood relationship, met and married; on discovering their twinship, they then divorced. Since then, there have been documentaries on the powerful and tragic nature of these experiences that result from what is called genetic sexual attraction that occurs between separated twins and siblings. These were represented in the tragic tale of the opposite sex twins Sigmund and Siglinde, the children of the god, Woton, represented in Wagner's opera *The Ring Cycle* (1870). They are separated in infancy and then, unwitting of their relationship, find each other and fall in love. It is not a new phenomenon.

There have been public expressions of compassion for the pain of these experiences along with expressions of primitive disgust. It is interesting to note that media and internet soft pornography supports the literature that, surprisingly, reports sexual fantasies and enactment between same sex twins more frequently than between opposite sex twins. This may be because same sex twins are researched much more. I believe there is a window here into knowledge that is beyond this project, but is part of the context of this research story. Attitudes towards adoption and fostering are beginning to change, moving towards a recognition of the damage caused by splitting twin or sibling groups. The importance of sibling relationships is at last being thought about. The definition of incest is being teased out. There is some discernment of difference between adult–child incest and consenting adult sibling–sibling incest, as long as it does not involve others or offspring. This book finds itself being part of the rising tide of interest and investigation into the nature of relationship experience for siblings, same sex twins, and opposite sex twins.

Interest in opposite sex twins is capturing not just the imagination of the public, but also that of science, education, and psychotherapy. Literature on twins by twins is rare, but twins who have made important contributions to the field are usually same sex twins: George Engel (1975), Joan Woodward (1998), Nancy Segal (1999), and Donna and Dorothy Davis (2004a,b). In 2000, when I started this research project, it was, to my knowledge, groundbreaking. There was no research on opposite sex twins by an opposite sex twin with a group of opposite sex twins. There was also no research that employed methods of psychodrama, painting, and reflection for data collection.

Culture

There are plays, operas, and films that give twins a significant role, although there are fewer involving opposite sex twins. Some of the most well known are *Twelfth Night* (Shakespeare, 1601); *The Dreamers* (Bertolucci, 2003), and *Festen* (Vinterberg, 1999).

There are a few novels in which opposite sex twins play a part, for example: *The Bridge of San Luis Rey* (Wilder, 1927); *The God of Small Things* (Roy, 1997); *The Sotweed Factor* (Barth, 1960). I found that, as I reflected on my research, the contributions in literature became quietly but increasingly significant. There were discrete remarks that I became aware of which seemed to match the research reflections. In *The Sotweed Factor*, Barth, an opposite sex twin himself, gave what appeared to be a small place to the twin sister of the main character, a poet. At the end of the book the twins were reunited and the importance of their twin relationship emerges. Perhaps this was possible because the book was set at the end of the seventeenth century, when there was an expectation that siblings would look after each other.

Around this time I saw several productions of *Twelfth Night*, a play whose central theme is around opposite sex twins. I found myself becoming increasingly aware of the possible dynamics of opposite sex twins in the family unconsciously expressed in this play. This was stimulated by the knowledge that Shakespeare was the father of opposite sex twins. His opposite sex twin son died aged eleven. *Twelfth Night* was written later, when his twin daughter was around the age of Viola, the opposite sex twin girl in the play. It seemed, therefore, that Shakespeare, as father, was working out his feelings about his twins. Why had I never really noticed before? It was as if the research immersion had given me a clearer vision, like infra-red goggles bringing into full awareness that which has always been there but not noticed. To find out if this new awareness had any validity for others, I started giving demonstration lectures to share and explore these insights that had emerged from the research and influenced my understanding of *Twelfth Night*. My expectation was that the audience would see this interpretation as fanciful, but it was not so. This surprised me.

There is a universal fascination with twins. Twins of all descriptions abound in myths and folk-tales. Freud described myths as the products of ethnic imagination (Freud, 1912–1913). Among these myths are those that the ten tribes of Israel are said to have descended from Jacob's ten sons, who each married their twin sisters (Sandbank, 1988); Narcissus was said to mourn the loss of his twin sister, not himself (Sandbank, 1999); Adam and Lilith, and then Adam and Eve, have been seen as twin-like (Lewin, 2004); Isis and Osiris were believed to have fallen in love in the womb (*ibid.*).

Myths have been handed down throughout time, despite the progress in knowledge in other domains such as history, archaeology, anthropology, sociology, science, and politics. It has been said that Greek mythology is considered to contain almost all there is to know of our unconscious internal relationship patterns (Anzieu, 1979). It tracks the development of the psyche, which includes a fascination with twins. Many people want an imaginary twin, of which sex I do not know. But the fascination with opposite sex twins and, therefore, an imagined opposite sex twin, is more complex. There seems to be a fear about how to relate to them. They stir up exciting and dangerous feelings around intimacy or incest and can ultimately be experienced as a threat to the species. Opposite sex twins have been revered or reviled in different societies. They have been killed (this can be due to shortage of milk in mothers who have a poor diet); or, conversely, made to marry, made into rulers, or deified (Lewin, 2004; Rosambeau, 1987; Sandbank, 1988). Much as Freud recognized the importance of myths as a part of our internal world which included siblings and twins (Freud, 1900a), until recently they were relegated to inhabiting the outer margins of mainstream psychoanalytical thought and theory of infant development (Lewin, 2004). Many a story from psychotherapy literature has been about a child and its parents. These seem to feature only children with no siblings. This absence of siblings in the stories is beginning to change.

The literature has progressed. It tends to group all twins together, although same sex twins have been far more widely researched. Grouping the twins together, to a certain extent, is justified. Twins of all kinds are a constant puzzle in the nature/nurture debate that ultimately impacts on many aspects of social encounter from the personal to the political. There are many ways in which opposite sex twins are like siblings, other twins, and even only children. These similarities and differences have been summed up in Chapter Eight.

Contemporary sciences

Scientific research has begun to make surprising discoveries about opposite sex twins that are challenging the paucity of thinking about them in psychotherapy. "Opposite sexers", as Barth (1960) calls them, are unseen twins so unlike identical same sex twins that they have been less noticed. They are presumed to be different, male and female, Venus (the goddess of love) and Mars (the god of war). This difference of gender is seen as apparent and familiar. However, for scientists, opposite sex twins have become a relatively recent source of fascination because of what they have begun to discover through them and the implications this has on our stereotypes of gender roles and identity. Twins are the living embodiment of what is truly other and what is self. In this twins can be a mirror of each other and for us all. There are intriguing scientific discoveries relevant to this book. As far as possible, I have set these out below chronologically. The subjects included are: types of twins, chimerism, birth rate, birth order, physical peculiarities with regard to health; longevity; eyesight; ear and jaw formation; resemblance to parents; and inter-uterine processes.

Twin types

There are two main twin types. Monozygotic twins develop from a single egg and sperm that then splits into two eggs. Dizygotic twins develop from two eggs, each fertilized by a different sperm. In either case, a zygote is a fertilized egg that may develop into an embryo in the first eight weeks after conception, during which time the structures and organs develop. Once these are distinctly formed, the zygote becomes a foetus and eventually emerges as the mature organism of a baby. The zygosity, or description of the DNA of the fertilized eggs of twins as monozygotic or dizygotic, is defined by blood, enzymes, protein types, and fingerprints. Opposite sex twins are generally seen to be dizygotic, but, curiously, they can be genetically nearer to monozygotic twins than same sex twins. Boklage holds that, while identical twins can be more distinct than can be imagined, fraternal twins might come from the same egg. There can even be opposite sex twins who are nearly monozygotic, but have different sex chromosomes. Bry (1999) sees this as unusual. Boklage (2005) has a special interest in chimerism. Chimerism is the presence of two different cell lines within an individual where the organism is composed of two genetically distinct types of cells that originate in different zygotes. In the case of opposite sex twins, chimerism can occur through blood exchanges in the womb. Chimerism is not the same thing as mosaicism. Mosaicism occurs when two different cell lines originate in the same person, due to a mutation or chromosomal error in early gestation (Segal, 2009). These are examples of the mysteries and variations of twin formation being discovered.

In the light of these scientific discoveries, Lewin (2004) describes the correlation between genetics and nurture that influence the lives of everyone. The environment moulds us and offers a continually changing spectrum of opportunities. Thus, the fields of science and culture appear to influence the development of opposite sex twins (Miller, 1994) and come together in the exciting field of neuro-psycho-biology. These have begun to unlock the relationship between the body, experience, and mind that validates the topic and methodology of this research. It is now known that learning takes place early on in the womb, and that each child has a genetic blueprint (Lewin, 1994).

We tend to think that either genetics or environmental influence has the upper hand but Segal (2009) holds that nor is it 50/50. This is really not quite correct—gene environment/contributions vary across traits—it could be 50–50 for some traits (personality) but more like 30–70 for job satisfaction and so forth.

Many couples find themselves unexpectedly pregnant with twins or multiples while others are surprised not to have them. So, how frequent is the incidence of twins?

Birth rates

The incidence of twins is changing within the overall birth rates. While beyond the remit of this research, it needs noting that, with over population, pollution, and the threat to the environment, birth rates are dropping significantly. Are humans, as a species, adapting to their changing environment? While birth rates are decreasing there are increasing numbers of twins and multiple births in the UK and elsewhere, although the rate of physical damage in the womb is far higher than for singletons. The twinning rate was 9.6 in 1980, compared to 15.1 in 2007. This trend has been rising in recent years, and the proportion of multiple births by age group is 6.3 in those under 20 years old, rising to 21.7 in 35–39-year-olds, and 56.7 in the over 45s (Kenneth, Kochanek, Joyce, & Martin, 2008). Women now choosing to have babies at a later age are prone to conceiving twins or multiples. *In vitro* fertilization (IVF) has also been influential in the increase of twins. In the UK today, about one in thirty-four babies are born as twins or triplets (in 1980 it was one in fifty-two). The worldwide rate of identical twinning has always been an inexplicable constant at three to four twins per 1000 births. Fraternal twinning, however, varies according to mother's age, twins on the female side of the family, and geography. Opposite sex twins are a third of all twin births (Bryan, 1983). It is recognized that more than 50% of infants start life as a twin in the womb (Rosambeau, 1987). Research has yet to establish whether there is a correlation between this phenomenon and how many people fantasize about having a twin (Zazzo, 1976).

The reality is that twins are on the increase. Attitudes towards child-rearing are changing at an alarming rate that may well result in a more frequent choice of opposite sex twins as a pragmatic approach to family-making through IVF. Angelina Jolie and Brad Pitt chose to have opposite sex twins. They are probably not the first, looking at the number of famous couples with opposite sex twins. Babies' DNA is being altered to make them how their parents want them. These incidences are over and above altered DNA for medical reasons. So, why not have fast-track family-making? Wisot (2008) observed that "We live in an era of reproductive freedom, so anybody can do anything they want within legal limits", so changing forever the place of conception in the human species.

Is this a marvel of humankind's making, a solution to female emancipation, or a travesty of our place in nature? These huge ethical issues are beyond the remit of this research, but cannot go unremarked in the context of this book. On the other hand, humankind's remarkable capacity to perform caesareans has saved the lives of many a mother and infant, but might also affect the significance of birth order for twins and their families. The possible ensuing role confusion described below is unquestionably second to that of the lives saved, but has its place in the twin field.

Birth order

The importance of birth order is of long standing in terms of status and expectation in the family, and therefore is important in birth order for all twins. The eldest is traditionally conferred family power and estate. It is, therefore, an economic and an emotional subject. Several views in the literature find that the first-born twin is often regarded with family favour, especially if he is a boy (Stuart, 2001).

However, in contrast to our Western assumptions, there are cultures that hold the interesting belief that the second-born is the deeper in the womb, therefore conceived first. In this role, they are the leader. They are seen to send the first-born out to investigate the world. The first-born twin is thought to be more lively and outgoing, while the second-born is cautious but wiser (Sandbank, 1988). This was news indeed for me, and gave a whole new perspective to the birth order question. I have now come across this tendency surprisingly often, so it seems that there is truth in both views. It is one of the many role confusions so prevalent in opposite sex twins, as revealed in the fascinating research of physical and psychological peculiarities of opposite sex twins.

Physical attributes

These researches peculiar to opposite sex twins include their health, longevity, eyesight, pelvis shape, ear shape, jaw size, and the tendency to be similar in appearance to their opposite sex parent.

For twins, in general, their health and longevity are more at risk than those of singletons. Miller (1994) observes that opposite sex twins appear to do rather better than same sex twins in terms of health and longevity. Stocks and Karns (1933), and later Koch (1955), find opposite sex twins have a higher rate of premature births. Poorer eyesight in premature babies also occurred where they were given oxygen. This poor sightedness is more apparent in opposite sex twins than same sex twins, who also tend to have a much higher rate of myopia or nearsightedness than singletons (Miller, 1994).

There are further peculiarities. Boklage (1985) examines asymmetry in dental diameters in twins. He is able to classify these dentures between male and female almost correctly. However, with opposite sex twins he misclassifies 70% of the males, and 90% of the females. McFadden (1993) then finds that opposite sex twin females emit far fewer continuous tones or hums in their ears compared with other females. These hums, called spontaneous auto-acoustic emissions (SOAE), are discharged by hair cells in the inner ear. The emissions raise the volume of weak sounds to make them audible. The limit of these hums in the ears of the opposite sex twin females are like those of their twin brother. In this specific respect, opposite sex twin females are "masculinized".

Opposite sex twins are defined by the genes of their father. This is so even if twins might have been conceived by two fathers, the mother having had more than one partner. It is indeed possible for a pregnant woman to conceive a second child during the early stages of her pregnancy (Sandbank, 1988). This discovery has been accompanied by an explosion of research, due to the invention of ultrasound. New ways of researching life in the womb has become possible and has altered perceptions of pre-birth experience forever.

In the womb

A growing number of questions can be asked about the physiology and health of same sex twins and opposite sex twins in and out of the womb. How is the psycho-biology of opposite sex twins similar to, or different from, twins or singletons? How do environmental harmonies and conflicts affect infants in the womb? These questions are addressed later in the book (Chapter Nine). Here, the question is, what are the discoveries that have been made about the transfer of hormones and neuro-chemicals between twins in the womb and what are their possible influences on the body, behaviour, and psyche of opposite sex twins (Miller, 1994)? There are different views on the transfer of hormones. Opposite sex twins make it possible for the exploration of hormone transfer to be worked through. It is thought that hormone transfer occurs from the male opposite sex twin foetus to the female opposite sex twin foetus, raising the level of testosterone and other male hormones in her. Female hormones are also thought to transfer to the opposite sex twin male (Mitchel, Baker, & Jacklin, 1989). Prenatal female hormones do not appear necessary for genital feminization in mammals and humans, but male hormones are necessary for masculinization. Sex related hormones are chemically quite similar to the hormone cortisol, which in itself is structurally similar to testosterone. Furthermore, if steroids and female hormones transfer through maternal and foetal circulations, it is very likely that they and male hormones also transfer from one foetus to another. Interestingly, Koch takes another view: that opposite sex twin females do not seem as masculinized by their brothers' influence as much as the brothers are feminized by theirs. This is seen as a social, rather than a hormonal, influence. Feminization, here, in contrast to the masculine influences, is defined by affectionateness, tenacity, obedience, cheerfulness, responsibility, and friendliness to children (Koch, 1966). The feminization of the male opposite sex twin, which Koch thought was neglected, is here redressed in recognition that hormone disposition within the opposite sex twins might influence their social behaviour.

Whatever the final outcome, scientists, such as Boklage, hold that if even a small part of the hormones from the opposite sex parent or twin reached the foetus, the quantity can be large relative to what is required for observable behavioural change in the small embryo. Thus, it seems that individuals with inadequate sex hormones might develop to be neither fully male nor fully female, and leave no descendants (Miller, 1994). This could threaten the survival of the species and validate the taboo of incest. However, the candle has been lit to allow us, with much excitement, to observe the mysteries of the womb. Through ultrasound twins can be seen kissing, punching and stroking each other. This in turn makes us wonder about the beginning of passion and other emotions.

The questions raised about hormones are complemented by the field of neuroscience. Stern, Bruschweiler-Stern and Freeland (1998), Schore (2001), Boadella (2001), Trevarthen (2003), and Watt (2003), among others, bring the relationship of the body and mind to our attention in the field of psycho-neurology. Schore (2001) describes the orbital frontal lobe of the cerebral cortex in the right hemisphere of the infant's developing brain as the senior executive of the social–emotional brain, through which it takes in relationship pre-symbolically. Towards the end of the second year, storing experience begins to develop as symbolic and representational. Thus, the primary object relationship is internalized and transformed into a psychic structure on a neurological base. The sympathetic and parasympathetic nervous systems are responsible for the expression of somatic states, and therefore the visceral (felt in the chest and abdomen) and somatic (the body) states process the self-related material represented in the right hemisphere. This theory of the brain informs, enlightens, and underpins psycho-dramatic practice of embodiment and metaphor through action, taking forward Freud's observation that "the ego is first and foremost a bodily ego" (Freud, 1923, p. 26).

Stern also describes the prenatal and postnatal interchanges between twins as based on their sensing rather than perceiving. This early inner–outer experience forms perception which develops into patterns of interpersonal relatedness. When the patterns then become enduring, they form the basis of character structure (Stern, 1985). Stern (1985) observes that, far from being an undiscriminating blob, each infant, twin, or singleton, responds uniquely to its environment and makes an impact upon it, even in the womb. Piontelli (2002) goes further, stating that the relationships after birth can mirror the relationship within the womb, both with their twin and their mother. These patterns of relating are different from singletons. Lewin (2004) holds that twins are always present for each other, whether in the womb or in the mother's mind. Davis and Davis (2004b), contend that, as identical twin women, they have always had a sense of themselves. They are aware of each other and their differences. It is others who cannot see them as they see themselves.

Opposite sex twins have been understood through their behaviour after birth, behaviour that can be influenced by biological as well as psychological factors (Miller, 1994). The biological factors that can affect the behaviour of opposite sex twins are researched through intelligence, verbal ability, spatial performance, perceptual speed, language, and sensation seeking.

Intelligence

Husen (1959) finds no difference in intelligence in opposite sex male twins and same sex male twins, but he finds that, in primary school, the opposite sex twin males do better in reading, writing, and history. Record, McKeown and Edwards (1970) find that having a twin brother appears to lower the female verbal ability by 43% towards the lower average ability of their male twin. This may be due to testosterone and brain masculinization. The other possibility can be that having a brother means studying harder. On the other hand, Fischbein (1978) finds that having a male twin appears to have a significant positive effect on female performance in mathematics. Fischbein also finds that a large difference between the sexes is in perceptual speed (speed of perception), in which females are superior. However, having a twin brother appears to shift the female score for perceptual speed to over halfway towards her male opposite sex twin's perceptual speed, so opposite sex twin girls score lower than other girls. Turning to spatial performance, Cole-Harding, Morstad and Wilson (1988) show that the scores for female twins are not significantly different from those of their twin brothers, suggesting that exposure to testosterone *in utero* improves spatial ability in females. This patterning is also seen in language development.

Language

The need for language with all twins is not of the same order as for singletons, so language tends to develop more slowly. This is attributed to the failure of bonding with the mother as a significant factor (Taubman-Ben-Ari, Findler, & Kuint, 2004). Language is being seen as the "social glue that replaced grooming" (Dunbar, 1996, p. 79). Slow language development in opposite sex twins is also seen to be due to higher levels of female hormones in the mothers (Tambyraja & Ratnam, 1981; Trapp, 1986). Language development has implications for education and socialization (Laffey-Ardley & Thorpe, 2006; Thorpe & Gardner, 2006). Slow language development can be particularly true of opposite sex twins, who might not compete with each other in a similar way to either same sex twins or other siblings. They also might not, for whatever reason, play together. Of the three pairs of opposite sex twins in my research, one pair is also dyslexic. Language, although only a small component of communication, is imperative, not just in educational tasks, but in all relationships, and can act as a regulator of behaviour. Furthermore, the behaviour of opposite sex twins does not appear quite as would be expected.

Behaviour

A puzzling outcome of research arises from Zazzo's observation that, in a number of characteristics, opposite sex twins appear to be less alike than "MZ twins but more alike than same sex twins" (Zazzo, 1960, p. 642). This is a finding he does not expect. Zazzo (1976) also finds that twins normally resembled the parent of their own sex, but that this was weaker in opposite sex twins. Opposite sex twin females resemble their fathers more closely than their mothers, while opposite sex twin males have only a slightly greater tendency to resemble their mothers. It appears to be understood that there is no resemblance to that parent in personality. But not so with *Twelfth Night*'s Sebastian (Viola's twin brother) who says of his twin sister: ". . . yet thus far I will boldly publish her: she bore a mind that envy could not but call fair . . .", while he described himself thus: "My bosom is full of kindness, and I am yet so near the manners of my mother that upon the least occasion more mine eyes will tell tales of me" (Shakespeare, 1601). This is upheld by Eysenck and Wilson (1979), who find that individuals with pelvises like those of their opposite sex parent tend to resemble that parent in behaviour. The implications of these findings are seen to affect behaviour and relationships.

Relationships

Research into opposite sex twins' relationships reveal surprising discoveries in their behaviour. These involve themes of dominance, popularity, socialization (learning how to relate), confusion of roles, as well as relationship difficulties for adolescence, marriage, and parenthood.

It seems that the female opposite sex twins are more affected by socialization than their male twins. Koch (1955) finds that twins spend a lot of time with each other, developing a special bond, and perhaps they come to think alike. This may cause opposite sex twin females to be more masculine in their opinions and opposite sex twin brothers to be more feminine. Most anecdotal stories of opposite sex twins describe the dominance of the female twin. Zazzo (1960) reports that, in 80% of opposite sex twins, the dominant twin is female and closer to father, although sometimes in competition with him. Opposite sex twins both appear to get on with mother. This does not seem to be influenced by birth order. Dominance of one twin appears to depend on the weight, height, and maturity of the boy and if the sons are more valued (Sandbank, 1999, p. 173). Koch (1955), and, later, Fischbein, Ove and Cenner (1991) also find opposite sex twin males are popular and opposite sex twin females are unusually unpopular. This surprising outcome may be due to the effects of hormone transfer already described. Miller (1994, p. 9) reports that "The opposite sex females, having been exposed to extra testosterone, would be less popular, while opposite sex males, having their testosterone partially off-set by female hormones, would be more popular than other males". However unbalanced the popularity is for the opposite sex twins, Koch finds a vocational correlation in the "striking divergence between the sexes when two groups, uniform in sex" are compared. However, this is "not apparent in the two sex groups derived from opposite-sex pairs" (Koch, 1966, p. 163).

The opposite sex twins of this research wanted to focus on their intimate relationships, as well as their own relationship. For all twins, there is a fear of being alone that can be greater than singletons, who may have developed the capacity for solitude. Be that as it may, feelings of the opposite sex twins can vary, like all siblings and same sex twins, from extreme love to extreme hate. There appears a possibility of social awkwardness in the opposite sex twin girls and popularity of the opposite sex twin boys. But, with many adolescent boys, the opposite sex twin boy may be shaken by the girl's faster maturation. Sandbank (1988) notes that many opposite sex twin boys led very independent lives and may have doubts about their own masculinity unless the girl was a late developer. Sandbank (1999) observes that there is a confusion of roles and role models for opposite sex twins, coupled with a relationship that in closeness appears to be more like same sex twin females than same sex twin males. The opposite sex twin female personality is more "like that of same sex twin girl film stars—used to attention" (Sandbank, 1999, pp. 74–75), who got on well with both parents, has a special relationship with one of them, and tends to want to be a twosome (Sandbank, 1988). Koch (1955) finds that these opposite sex twin sisters are more competitive, ambitious, enthusiastic, and less wavering in decisions, and are less likely to build alibis and to be more tenacious of purpose than children with sisters. Comparison of the behaviour of opposite sex twin females to same sex twin females also shows that the opposite sex twin females have a significant increase in sensation-seeking, disinhibition, thrill-seeking, and adventure, like males (Resnick, Gottesman, & McGue, 1993). So this, along with male hormones, may go some way to explain the possible lack of popularity in childhood of these opposite sex twin girls.

Byng-Hall (1995) finds that twins tend to marry someone with a personality similar to their twin, although parents, brothers, and sisters are sometimes used as models. Relationships might be influenced not just by family patterns, but also by the pattern of the twinship. Further to this, Sandbank (1999) warns the opposite sex twin female to be "on her guard against over-protecting her partner while the opposite sex twin male may look for a strong partner on whom he can depend" (ibid., p. 183). During the research, I was surprised to find a frequent anecdote regarding the father's difficulty with his opposite sex twin boy. Is there a social reason as to why the opposite sex twin boys appear to need to be protected by mother? The fathers appear to prefer the opposite sex twin girls. What is the impact on a father who might feel he has lost his wife to his son and then finds he has also lost his twin daughter to the same son? The confusion of roles might not just belong to the opposite sex twins, but to the parents as well, and might contribute to opposite sex twins being at greater risk as adults of psychiatric disorder, compared to singletons and other twin types (Klaning, Bo Mortensen, & Ohm Kyvik, 1996).

This section has looked at the drama created between the knowledge of some physical peculiarities and neuro-biology of opposite sex twins and how they interweave with their behaviour and relationships. This scientific drama illustrates the remarkable way in which the body and mind are intertwined. However, to complete this intertwining, the threads of knowledge about human unconscious processes need to be described from the literature of psychotherapy that has enhanced and challenged my research.

Contemporary psychotherapy

Psychoanalytic theory

As described in the Introduction, current psychotherapy literature centres around the theories of personality development that generate from the primary relationship of infant and mother. This relationship is seen to be crucial to the development of the infant's sense of self. It has been, therefore, the major influence on psychotherapy practice for the past century. With a sense of self, the infant can have the psychic strength to weather the Oedipal experience of triangular relationships. The triangular relationship develops when a second adult, traditionally understood as the father figure (Lewin, 2004), enters into the mother–child relationship. This next major relationship development is also seen as crucial to psychic development. As will be seen in Chapter Three, these maturational processes develop the internal–psychic relationship experience that facilitates social engagement and leads to shared relationships with parents, siblings, and peers.

Family therapy theory

Psychoanalytic principles, preoccupied with the problems within the individual, are challenged by the systemic theory of family therapy that perceives problems as belonging to the family group. There are other significant paradigms. Aries (1962) is not alone when he sees the child as a historical construct. Hartmann (1952), Abrams and Neubauer (1994), Mitchell (2003), and Lewin (2004) hold that the presence of a silent inherent blueprint influences the unfolding of the human mind. Smith (1988) weaves the nature/ nurture issue neatly together by defining heredity as the provider of a physiology that allows for creative, flexible individuals. Bainham, Day Sclater, Richards and Cambridge Socio-Legal Group (1999) expand these approaches. If the child is a historical construct, so, then, must be the parents, as a part of that chain of historical construction. Schutzenburger (1998) also describes how the elements of relationship fusion can be trans-generational, and may pass through the parents and the parental relationship itself to the grandchildren. It is not exactly understood how this phenomenon happens as yet, but it is endorsed by the observations of others, some of whom have been mentioned. Schore (2001) puts all the ideas together. He describes how attachment depends on a geneti-cally encoded psycho-biological predisposition, the experience of the primary care-giver, and by the life experiences of other family members, siblings, or twins.

Contributors to the knowledge of twins

Contemporary psychotherapy theory has seen significant contribu-tions on the role of siblings and twins from Bryan (1983), Sandbank (1988), Piontelli (2002), Mitchell (2003), Coles (2003), and Lewin (2004). Their work forms the backbone of this part of the literature review. There are relatively few papers in psychotherapy on the topic of twins. The papers most quoted are by Burlingham (1952); Bion (1967); Bick (1968); Zazzo (1976); Stern (1985); Athanassiou (1986); Sheerin (1991); McDonald (2001); Kruger (2001); Marsdon (2001); Swanson (2001); Coles (2003); Mitchell (2003); Segal, Hersberger and Arad (2003); Lewin (2004); and Penninkilampi-Kerola, Kaprio, Moilanen, Ebeling and Rose (2004). They express sensitive and significant contributions to the understanding of twins. The themes that they raise, important to this research, start with the development of the twins' infant experience of their psychic skin, the importance of infant regulation, and the Oedipal stage. These are followed by discussions on the significance of the family dynamics, fighting and discernment, fantasies and incest, and healthy and unhealthy twinning.

Psychic skin

The psychic sense of self, and, therefore, the body boundaries within each twin infant, raise concern in the literature. Body boundary results in what Bick (1968) calls "psychic skin" that can in turn give rise to fantasies of internal and external space that influence the experience of the self. This delicate metaphor of psychic skin can describe what happens between the twins when the integrating object of mother is lacking or absent. The internalization of the twin as a primary object is seen to lead to a lack of an adequately developed individual skin in the very small infant. Bick (1986) and later Proner (2000) express anxieties around the early unintegrated state of the babies, prior to a sense of self and with insufficient psychic skin. This can lead to a catastrophic experience defended against through a second false skin or self. This means that the skin between the twins is thin while the skin around the twin pair is thick because regulation with an adult has been insufficient (Meltzer 1975).

Regulation

Regulation is reached, Schore (1996) suggests, through empathy, a non-verbal psycho-biological attunement, which Proner (2000) describes as a synchronised dance between mother and infant. This dance is at the heart of the early psycho-biological and self-regulatory system in the brain called the cortico-limbic system that is the vital neurological substrata of the unconscious. The system is regulated by the mother. How does mother regulate? She regulates the infant's production of neuro-hormones and hormones that influence the activation of gene action systems by the way she responds and engages with her baby. These systems programme the structural growth of the brain regions essential to future socio–emotional relationships. This is done through touch, voice, eye contact, and empathy, helping the infant to modulate emotion. It is play. Warm and happy feelings, the desire to hold, touch, and nurse the pain of separation and the joy and excitement of reunion, all have neurochemical correlates that allow the experience of wonderful feelings. Through a biochemical cascade, mother–child interactions stimulate the secretion of oxytocin, prolactin, endorphins, and dopamine, which create positive and rewarding feelings. Cozolino (2002) describes how the infant learns to regulate emotional arousal through this dance with mother. Twins are perceived to be unable to provide regulation for each other. Furthermore, it is understood that they could indeed cause each other to become overwhelmed with emotion. This could be frightening for the little ones.

Regulation is complex with twins. Unlike the first-born child, after birth the infant twins face two opposing maternal images: a mother, who through her containment of the twin, can aid development but the same mother, who in so doing, also interferes in the twinship (Burlingham, 1952). Athanassiou (1986) describes a disturbing picture of the twin baby at the breast sensing the rage of the excluded other twin baby, so poisoning its own experience of the breast that can then create a parasitic relationship between them. There are others (pp. 25, 27, 28) who express similar concern for unconscious processes that could be destructive. A twin is never alone with mother: even when the other baby is asleep, it is still in mother's mind. I surmise that each baby also has a body sense of the other twin, even if not conscious or symbolized in the mind. Davison (1992) suggests the merging of the breast twin with the actual twin can become an internal structure. There is also the possibility that inter-twin rivalry might even lead to an anti-symbiotic trend with the mother. The mother can be in tension about saving one twin from another, but my position is that neither exclusion of twin or mother is a psychic option. Complex as this dance may be, the triangulation of *one and one make three* is recognized and understood by McDonald (2001), Mitchell (2003), Sandbank (1988), and Lewin (2004).

In contrast to these possible difficulties, Piontelli (2002) watches twin babies who appear content with their twin. Stern (1985) suggests that each twin could be, for the other, an aspect of their environment that gradually acquires the characteristics of a core "other" as a mental representation of intersubjective experience after the first seven months (Davison, 1992). It is my view that, happy or hateful as twinship may be, there is "sense-knowledge" before thought that is beginning to be recognized. Even mother may be second to the twinship if she cannot embrace them both in her mind.

Audrey Sandbank, the mother of same sex female twins, described to me that she felt she could never get into her twins. My reply was that she could never get out. Perhaps both statements are true.

Parental intervention

Be that as it may, regulation and parental intervention in the twin-ship is seen as of major importance in the creation of an adequate space for each twin. Parents and twins become significant internal figures. Recently, I was told of a physical manifestation of this. A baby opposite sex twin girl had physical problems that seem to be derived from her brother having squashed her stomach in the womb. However, the only way the father could comfort his scream-ing daughter was to lay the boy on top of her again. Was this a physical representation of regulation that was not just between parent and child, but also between the opposite sex twins?

Dibble and Cohen (1981) view the parents' attitude to be as influ-ential even from before the birth of the twins as it is after. For ex-ample, after birth there can be a parental reluctance to interfere or intervene with the twins. Parents need to be able to manage their own Oedipal and sibling relationships so that they can help their twins in the processes of discernment. The mother's capacity to tolerate her own feelings of being left out is an essential element in helping the infant twins deal with feelings evoked in an inherently triangular situation (Davison, 1992). Sometimes, twins resist parents' interference by splitting mechanisms through a division of qualities rather than true differences in themselves (Lewin, 2004). This can maintain a lack of regulation and discernment and, therefore, spon-taneity and creativity in the pre-Oedipal stage of infant develop-ment. Nothing in nature is that tidy in terms of stages, but the next stage of infant development is known as the Oedipal stage.

The Oedipal stage

The Oedipal stage is where the child confronts the parent of the same sex for the superior position with the parent of the opposite sex. The boy challenges the father so that he can seduce the mother. The girl hopes to seduce the father from the mother. Powerful as the feel-ings are, the child has to lose the struggle if they are to internalize a triangle of relationships in which all three, mother, father, and child, have a place. If this relinquishment is not reached, the child will be trapped in a claustrophobic duo with a possibly possessive parent of the opposite sex, in which the parent of the same sex is seen as the bad object. This can mean that there appears to be no rescue. The misery of the situation can be sexualized, in fantasy if not in fact, and guilt follows. This can have serious future implications for the child's relationships with siblings and peers. It is my experience that people caught in this trap often have few friends and regard siblings as insignificant to them. This is indeed a lonely place. People's mental health is most at risk when they are social isolates. Engel, a same sex twin, notes that the "difficulty of engaging with the Oedipal conflict" (Engel, 1975, p. 9) is more complex if it has not been resolved in either or both of the parents. The Oedipal stage, or struggle for recognition, represents what Lacan calls the "law of the Father" (Mitchell, 2003, p. 43): the fear of castration for the boy, or loss of love for the girl. Mitchell proposes that the Oedipal conflict can be displaced into the twin relationship to avoid the vertical child–parental relationship struggle. There are other considerations that are beyond the remit of this short overview on the unconscious processes of the Oedipal conflict. However, the review demonstrates the importance of this pivotal maturational experience that needs to be resolved to become internalized as a useful structure for future relationships.

Theory has tended to focus on the centrality of the Oedipal complex. Freud (1900a) interprets sibling, and, therefore, twin, relationships as re-enactments of the parents' relationship or the fantasized parent–child relationship. He sees these as an extension of the Oedipal situation and, therefore, one of rivalry for the parent of the opposite sex. However, Lacan (1993), Coles (2003), and Mitchell (2003) argue for the place of the twins to be firmly within the earlier pre-symbolic, imaginary realm, as an aspect of the pre-Oedipal stage of attachment. Mitchell (2003), advocating a more central role for siblings in developmental theory, cites earlier writers debating this subject. The anthropologist, Bronislaw Malinowski, argued that sibling relationships might be more important than parental relationships, whilst Ernest Jones, one of Freud's followers, asserted the universal centrality of "the totems and taboos on child–mother incest and child–father murder (the so called Oedipus complex) for the construction of all human culture" (Mitchell, 2003, p. x).

Family dynamics and siblings

While these unconscious processes are being worked through, they are affected by the interesting tendency of fathers of twins to handle firmly the non-identical and opposite sex twin boys (Sandbank, 1988). Although these twins are different, he treats them in the same way, while mother parents them differently from each other and is close to them both. The father can feel marginalized. These boys can lack confidence. Furthermore, opposite sex twin boys tend to be home-loving and in need of encouragement to tackle new tasks.

The importance of family dynamics and sibling relationships in personality development has become increasingly recognized. It follows on from there that "an examination of the general nature of twinning as experienced by and exacerbated in actual twins" (Lewin, 2004, p. 1) can lead to a greater understanding of developmental processes with both singletons and twins. The role of siblings is understood by Mitchell (2003), Coles (2003), and Lewin (2004) as essential in their influence on future intimate adult peer and marital relationships. Coles (2003) highlights how sibling love has been ignored and tends to be seen as a replacement of the child–parent relationship, not as love in its own right. Sibling relationships can facilitate the child's relationship development and their role repertoire. This expanding role repertoire influences the nature of the child's peer relationships and, hence, future adult relationships. But sibling relationships have their own set of trials that have to be overcome. Coles encapsulates how this role development is learnt by traversing intense and powerful feelings evoked by sibling experiences: "Sibling cruelty seems to eat into the psyche with a ferocity that is commensurate with the actual experience and gives a different twist to the harsh super ego" (Coles, 2003, p. 94). A harsh superego she sees as developing from unresolved sibling relationships. Mitchell (2000) describes siblings as the first social relationship in which the meaning of hatred and emptiness, as an expression of loss of place, has to be weathered. The birth of a sibling can give a child an experience of neglect that can lead to a catastrophic sense of displacement and to the wish to replicate oneself, which can lead to murderous feelings. The loving side of sibling relationships can mask the child's struggle with their experience of displacement. This struggle, known as the Antigone complex, is a life and death conflict with the arrival of their new sibling (Sandbank, 1999). Mitchell (2003, p. 43) sees that "the law of the Mother", as container, is needed to intervene at the level of sibling murderousness and incest so that the child's self can be restored. Dalal (1998) draws our attention to the importance of sibling/peer relationships that can give rise to or strengthen a *we* ego. The *we* ego can only be learnt through sibling/peer encounters. This has social and political implications, especially, at the time of writing, in view of the sharp rise in youth knife crime.

The Antigone complex (Mitchell, 2003) can be in opposition to the powerful and universal urge towards twinning; or are they two sides of the same coin? Many people want or create an imaginary twin (Klein, 1986). Twins also have imaginary twins (Bion, 1967). Twins can seek twinship in their external relationships (Sandbank, 1999), which can or cannot be a sign of their unresolved twin relationship. This imagined love object is understood not to be wanted as an object in itself, but for the purposes of identification and to receive love.

To take the nature of love further, Winnicott (1990) and Mitchell (2000) describe love as a positive emotion that comes about when there is no threat to survival. Coles comments that it does not follow that the intrinsic nature of sibling relationships is predicated upon displacement. She sees sibling love often expressed through the encounter between little people who beam at other little people, and notes that "siblings smile at each other more, intuitively pick up the feelings of the other sibling more quickly, and when they are separated they could experience intense feelings of loss" (Coles, 2003 p. 85). Cozolino (2002) also describes how the infant shares warm and happy feelings with other little people, and this can operate in the same biochemical cascade as the mother–child inter-action described in the section titled "Regulation". These relation-ships matter. It is recognized that sibling–peer (and, therefore, twin) relationships are not given up in the same way as parent–child rela-tionships, because they are part of their peer generation. Different roles, the many varieties of *us*, continue to develop through social networking with siblings and peers as well as with relating to older and younger generations. Thus, the network brings about a wide relational base to provide further external and internal balance to emotional arousal, spontaneity, and creativity. If regulation is lack-ing, twins and siblings could reach for other roles as a defence, such as being surrogate parents or teddy bears.

Twins and siblings as surrogate parents

Parens (1988) and Coles (2003) observe that twins can function in the parental role when there is, or appears to be, insufficient adult care. "Older siblings were often put out by the twins arrival and either became the negative attention seeker or became the surrogate parent of the twins" (Sandbank, 1999, p. 175). Siblings who feel jealous, anxious, or murderous can sometimes offset these feelings by choosing themselves, or being selected, as a substitute for mother in an attempt to compensate for the loss or absence of her (Lewin, 2004). So, with siblings or twins, they "may become an alternative base with the danger (particularly with boy/girl twins) of one twin, or sometimes both, attempting to take on the mantle of mother at an early age" (Sandbank, 1999, p. 168). Twins as parents, having had little experience of a one-to-one parent–child relationship, tend to fall into a child–child relationship, or group their children into pairs and not see that they need separate parental time. Many twin parents relate to one of the children as if they were their own twin. The mothers of mixed sex twins can be over protective towards their sons, but encourage independence in their daughters (Sandbank, 1988). This is not the only way in which twins and siblings seek out roles to contain their frightened and murderous feelings.

Teddy bears

It can happen that their twin becomes the primary object, or most important relationship, while the mother occupies a secondary position (Abraham, 1953). Sandbank (1999) describes this relationship as the making of the twin into a transitional object, like a teddy bear. What do teddy bears provide? They are the ones who know and hear secrets; get cuddled, hit, flung across the floor, and retrieved for reparation. The teddy bear can comfort the little infant twin in terms of survival and fantasy, but it cannot enlighten their understanding and toleration of relationships and so help to regulate the growing mind. The impact on the teddy bear twin may be that they, too, are at risk for themselves if they also get trapped in that role or trap their twin in that role. This fascinating metaphor seems to capture an intimacy of twins but it also seems to suggest that only one of the twins is a teddy bear. Is this because one twin is generally stronger than the other? Could it be they are both teddy bears to each other at the same time in their attempt to contain chaos? As already mentioned, they are capable of doing the opposite and winding each other up. So, like the role of surrogate mothers, teddy bears have their limits. At worst, they can become dependent on the other twin for the role of self. This self is understood as a false self, due to an inadequate secure base for their emotional–cognitive development. From this, the twins develop a limited capacity for symbol formation (Bowlby, 1988), which is essential for the creation of a relational internal world. The management of this internal world is predicated on the regulation of aggression and rivalry, so the teddy bear role has a place but does not become the only twin role.

Fighting and discernment

Because twins are the same age, rivalry between them can be more acute than between single siblings. Burlingham (1952) describes neither twin allowing him/herself to succeed for fear that they would be attacked by their twin. Twins usually adapt to the conflicts between each other and adjust to the personality of the other twin (Burlingham, 1952). Being an opposite sex twin can be less of a threat to identity than being a same sex twin. For opposite sex twins, the twinship can also appear to be less important, but some opposite sex twins forge strong links. Engel experienced the enduring nature and the narcissistic gains of twinship by "aggression between twins being dealt with by a delicate balance of the defences" (Engel, 1975, pp. 34–35). Siemon (1980), another same sex twin, suggests that there can be an experience of conflict and a fear of it. Sandbank (1999) holds that opposite sex twins fight little, or, if they fight, they can be more ferocious than other twins. The twins can thus damage themselves in anticipation, so "Fighting others is seen as a solution so as to not fight each other" (Lewin, 2004, p. 44).

While fighting is problematic for opposite sex twins, separation from a twin can be of a different order than from a parent. This may be because there is never a full share of mother. The nature of full share with mother is of a different order to that of a singleton. For a twin to have their full share of mother is to kill the other twin in the mind. This could be desirable, but catastrophic, as so many lone twins bear witness to (Hayton, 2007). I came to understand through my research that the only experience of full share for twins, in terms of a one-to-one relationship, is that experienced in the womb. This might be why it is easier to contemplate aggression than intimacy between siblings and twins, and especially opposite sex twins, as they inevitably raise sexual fantasies and concern about incest.

Fighting between opposite sex twins does not appear to happen physically, nor does sex, beyond the normal doctor and nurses games in childhood. Opposite sex twins do not have the need to fight for supremacy as they are not compared. They do not learn the strength from this "role", as they cannot compete. Family love of the boy is not the same as love for the girl. Neither of them can win, although the boys tend to be favoured over the girl. This fits with the cultural view that boys are more important than girls.

Fantasies and incest

Incest is, unsurprisingly, a central taboo around opposite sex twins. However, unlike parent–child incest, a degree of childhood sexual exploration and experimentation is tolerated or even permitted in different families and cultures. On the other hand, where sexual relationships between siblings are regarded as taboo they could be seen to become compulsive when linked with anxiety and feelings of guilt. Klein (1932) holds that fantasies underlying incestuous activity in children can shape the nature of their future sexual encounters. Sexual fantasies and incest are deeply embedded in the unconscious. Psychoanalytic theory argues that these fantasies can be towards sexually impulsive twinships as well as to the parents and their sexual relationship. The sexual fantasies of twins are seen as a refuge for the more narcissistic, or falling in love with the self, aspects of twin relationship. Some hold that the myth of Narcissus is that he is mourning the loss of his twin sister. Further interpretations suggest that twins, like their siblings, can use incestuous activity to ward off Oedipal fears of sex with a parent and to delay the resolution of the Oedipal conflict (Coles, 2002; Engel, 1975). Parens (1988) agrees with Freud that incest is an expression of the greater threat of fantasized parental incestuous gratifications. In contrast, Luzes (1990) suggests that it is incestuous love between siblings that is at the heart of sexual attraction rather than the triangular Oedipal drama with father and mother. Mitchell (2000) echoes

Luzes in viewing brother–sister incest as pre-Oedipal and therefore dyadic in nature. Mitchell (2003) views siblings' sex to be about life and death, not about sexual differences between the siblings. "Both the act and emotions of sex and of murderousness are for the same person" (Mitchell, 2003, p. 23). Sibling sex is not about sexual difference and, therefore, reproduction. These sexual acts are to make the other the same as the self so separateness does not have to be negotiated. One same sex twin, who was attending a transgender group, told me he found its membership did not include opposite sex twins, but same sex twins. How is this to be understood in regard to theories of incest? Mitchell holds that libidinal attachment between twins can be enacted in both heterosexual and homosexual activity. Fantasies and incest as an expression of the unconscious is a huge subject, here only touched upon, and will be returned to in Chapter Eight. These fantasies are also perceived to be a part of healthy or unhealthy twinning, depending on the life experiences of the opposite sex twins and on the culture in which these twins live.

Healthy and unhealthy twinning

Kohut (1971) distinguishes between normal and pathological twinning. He sees normal twinning as a need based on the experience of the presence of essential likeness, the self-affirming and self maintaining experiences of early childhood that are important in enabling a sense of belonging and participation. This healthy twinning can involve Klein's (1963) view that the breast is an imaginary twin in order to feel known, to belong, and to mitigate essential loneliness in early twin infancy. On the other hand, there are descriptions of problematic attachment behaviour in early infancy as a response to fear of separation and mutilating psychic damage in the twins (Lacombe, 1959) where one twin can become incomplete without the other. These attachments have been called an adhesive twinship (Glenn, 1966, Meltzer, 1975); an enmeshed twinship, projecting or imagining their feelings to be in the other twin (Maenchen, 1968); and a parasitic twinship, where one twin may have an advantage over the other (Rosenfeld, 1971). Athanassiou (1986) suggests that parasitism, or the clinging of one twin to the other twin, is based on the twins taking up opposite positions.

However, with regard to maternal care, the problem for a twin is that of a deficit in development, not a conflict (Lacombe, 1959). They do not get enough from adults in every way. They are short on the eye contact, gazing, being fallen in love with, touch, playing, and attention given to a single child. They can be seen as a mirror image of each other and forever paired. This can affect their strategies for coping. They can cut off from unwanted aspects of the self and avoid integrating them. They can task share as another solution. This is called the couple effect (Sandbank, 1999; Zazzo, 1976). The twins can join together against the outside world either by operating in the same or opposite ways. One twin tends to be active, the other passive, and this is reversible (Lewin, 2004). As a result of the experience of being a twin, a *weself* system of two personalities can function as one instead of an individual *I* identity. The twinship can overwhelm individuation (Ortmeyer, 1970). Twin refuge can be a psychic retreat (Steiner, 1993). Thus, twinship can be seen as a possible narcissistic refuge from the process of separation with mother or twin and again an avoidance of the space needed for the development of symbolic thought that has to be learnt through frustration (Lewin, 2004). The complexity of being an opposite sex twin is matched by the tussle for the carers to orchestrate the developing psyches of their infant twins.

This literature review has highlighted the powerful contributions made to the field that are relevant to this book. It does no more than touch the tip of the iceberg, but attempts to illustrate some of the scientific, behavioural, neuro-biological, analytic, and systemic perspectives relevant to opposite sex twin relationship experiences as well as theories of psychotherapy around infant development, maternal attachment, psychic skin, regulation, the Oedipal stage, family dynamics, fighting and discernment, fantasies and incest. It closes with processes of healthy or unhealthy twinning. The essence of these understandings here described will be discussed in relationship to the findings in this research in Chapter Nine.

CHAPTER TWO

The research project.
Who was involved?

CAPTAIN: It is perchance that you yourself were sav'd.
VIOLA: Oh my poor brother! And so perchance may he be.

(Shakespeare, *Twelfth Night*, 1601, 1.11: 5–7)

The previous chapter set the context of the knowledge in science, behaviour, and psychotherapy to which this research belongs. This chapter describes the participants in this research: three pairs of opposite sex twins, the cameraman, and my personal and professional roles. I found a small group of three adult pairs of opposite sex twins by word of mouth. I had had a range of responses that led me to reflect that perhaps the capacity of pairs of opposite sex twins to attend the research project was influenced by how they were feeling about themselves at the time. There were twins who did not want to be part of the research, or only one of the twins was interested in participating. For some the timing was not good.

It cannot go unmentioned that many opposite sex twins hate each other, hate being related, hate being hated, and hate being a twin. They feel alone and that does not fit, so they fight by keeping a distance. Operating as individuals raises hateful feelings of guilt and discomfort towards themselves as opposite sex twins and towards their twin, by whom they may also feel the most deeply known. Their bodies know. This hatred is often expressed by living on the other side of the world. It does not work. It leaves holes in their souls. Hatred is mostly constituted from fear of not belonging or fears of being engulfed. I have met many more opposite sex twins who do not want to know about this research than those who do.

This chapter describes the people involved in this research. A brief description is given of the three pairs of opposite sex twins who made the research possible. There was also a cameraman/film editor, without whom the film would not have been possible. The group wanted him to attend the workshops and not to be restricted to being called into the research activities solely when the film cassettes needed changing. He was imagined by the group to be my twin or my partner. Was this to help the twins feel less conscious, to see me coupled as a twin, a parent, or both? I did not know. I end this chapter by describing my personal role as an opposite sex twin and my professional motivation that influenced this book.

Outline of the three pairs of opposite sex twins in this research (Figure 1)

The pen outlines are visual images to accompany the verbal pictures of the three pairs of opposite sex twins. These are brief, so that the telling of their stories can belong to the opposite sex twins themselves as the book progresses. Their fuller family stories can be read in Chapter Seven. Although the research workshops took place in 2001–2002, their stories are told in the present tense.

The opposite sex twins are here identified as Carl and Clare, Joan and Jim, and Diana and Dan. These disguised names make it easier to see how the opposite sex twins communicate with each other and how they communicate with other members of the group. Their ages are strangely uniform: thirty-six, forty-seven, and fifty-seven at the time of the research.

● *Carl and Clare are forty-seven*
Carl teaches, builds, and gardens. Clare is a dentist. While the family was from the north of England, they grew up in New Zealand where

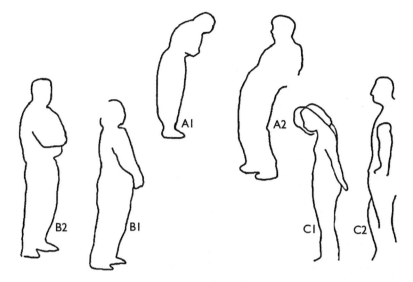

Figure 1. Outline picture of the opposite sex twins.

their father, mother, elder brother, elder sister, and their families continue to live. They both still visit their home and Carl tends to go back and forth more than Clare. Carl and Clare are both tall, attractive, giggly, and friendly. Carl likes a pint. They are the least experienced in talking about themselves. At the time of the research, Carl is living with Clare, looking after the house while she goes to work. He takes short-term work. He is single, while Clare has a very part-time partner. Carl loves gardening. Clare seems to have a lot of responsibilities setting up her own business. They are both very aware of appearing and behaving like the parent of the opposite sex in looks and personality.

● *Joan and Jim are fifty-seven*
Joan works with children with severe disability and Jim is an agricultural consultant. Joan lives with her family of five children. Her husband works abroad. The longest time he has been away is a year. Jim is in his second marriage, with two sons, in a small house in which they seem to stay close together. One set of grandparents were gypsy, for whom land was very important. The other grandfather was a jewellery-maker from a large East End of London family. Joan is an energetic, forthright, intelligent woman, and Jim

is articulate and eager. He is taller than she. They do not look alike. He appears more relaxed. They are both very attentive. Often, she initiates conversation or action. She appears to be outgoing in relation to other people while he appears to need to be understood by other people. Jim has been in psychological treatment and alternative medicine. Joan loves music and her girl-friends. Jim is concerned about where the next job will come from.

● *Diana and Dan are thirty-six*

Diana is an organizational manager; Dan is in media. They are attractive and well educated, like their two sisters, both of whom have children. Diana has her own children, a girl and boy whom she says she treats somewhat like twins. She is a single parent. Diana and Dan have a history of addiction and psychotherapy. Dan is gay, and also often single. He does a great deal of travelling. His work is his main hobby, while Diana loves culture and philosophy. They both have lots of friends from all walks of life.

My role as an opposite sex twin

I myself am an opposite sex twin, a role that perplexed me even though I spent many years in analysis from which I benefited enormously. But I can now see that, at that time, I could not reflect on the phenomenon of being an opposite sex twin. In 1998, as I ended my analysis, I carved the Triangle sculpture (Figure 2). I thought it represented my success in separating from my twin to fit in with the philosophy of individualism. This sculpture consisted of three heads, surrounded by two dolphins that were like arms around the figures.

Two years into the research, I suddenly realized that the metaphor of the peacock, seen at the back, was the unacknowledged twin. It was carved in relief, unlike the other three-dimensional figures (Figure 3).

I marvelled that what I had created was ahead of what I was able reflect upon. This embodiment was endorsed by a painting of twins I had made as an eight-year-old child that had surprisingly reappeared around that time (Figure 4).

These artistic endeavours were to determine painting as part of the research data. The use of a non-verbal medium would challenge

Figure 2.   My triangular sculpture.

Figure 3.   The back of my triangular sculpture.

Figure 4.   My painting of opposite sex twins.

the action of the research on the one hand that in turn would be challenged by reflection on the other. With the notion of this triangular structure, the doors to reflection on opposite sex twinship opened. The shame lifted as I started to wonder not just about me, but about how others felt being an opposite sex twin. I had never knowingly discussed the phenomenon of being an opposite sex twin with another opposite sex twin. During this time, my professional experience was also influencing my decision to undertake this research.

My professional role

I am a senior trainer and psychotherapist in psychodrama. The professional motivation to do the research arose from my work in a psychiatric hospital, where I ran open psychodrama groups for inpatients and day patients as part of the generic team. We had started to encounter an increase in the number of twins accessing the service. During supervision, my colleagues and I seemed unable to fathom the "hugeness" and the complexities of these twin patients. The analytic theory seemed to lack something. I felt my intuitions regarding our twin patients were going against the grain.

About this time I met Audrey Sandbank, the principal family therapy consultant for the Twin and Multiple Birth Association (TAMBA). She impressed me with her observations on opposite sex twins. I now knew I was on to something. I went to the International Society for Twin Studies (ISTS) 2001 conference, where the president at that time, Professor Louis Keith, and Dr Elizabeth Bryan, the previous president, confirmed that there was little research on opposite sex twins in psychotherapy. I was unable to find much to read on the psyche of opposite sex twins, and nothing that was written by opposite sex twins. The task, I decided, was mine. In undertaking such research, I hoped that it would bring transformation and understanding that might grow into personal and professional knowledge.

CHAPTER THREE

The philosophy of spontaneity

SEBASTIAN: She is drowned sir, with salt water, though I
seem to drown her remembrance again with more.

(Shakespeare, *Twelfth Night*, 1601, 11.1: 31–32)

The underlying philosophy of spontaneity and creativity
sustain and illuminate the visceral, or body-felt, knowledge
of unconscious choices in this research. In this chapter, I set
out to clarify why and how spontaneity is the underlying philosophy of my research design and what steps I took to validate it
through transcendental phenomenological methodology. As a
psychodramatist, I learnt the philosophy of spontaneity from the
works of Jacob Levy Moreno (1889–1974), who grew up and trained
as a psychiatrist in Vienna. He was directly and indirectly influenced by the ferment of change in his own contemporary environment of Vienna in the early twentieth century. Moreno was full of
other creative ideas, including a children's theatre, a theatre of
spontaneity for adults, encounter groups, group psychotherapy,
encounter groups. He was one of the pioneers of group psychotherapy. All of his innovations influenced the development of new

paradigms of modern social psychology. His major works are *Who Shall Survive* (1934), and *Psychodrama* Volumes I–III (1946). He is most quoted from *The Words of the Father* (1941). He read avidly, and turned to Greek philosophy and theatre to understand the healing power of emotion.

Moreno wanted to work with the socio-political dimensions of human suffering through facilitating spontaneity and creativity. He rejected the medical model of control and the analytic model that placed the cause of human misery at the door of humankind's destructiveness. For this purpose, Moreno wanted to develop a method for society as he wanted to treat society. Sociometry and sociodrama, the drama of the social experience, were dimensions of this purpose, and psychodrama set about resolving the ills of the individual. All these innovations were part of his grand design that saw the human being as a biological, psychic, familial, social, political being integrated by a cosmic role (Holmes, 1992). This was Moreno's political position. He invented different structures designed to explore, express, rehearse, and train spontaneity. These overarching structures are:

- sociometry—the mapping of group relationships;
- the theatre of spontaneity—the representation of the daily news;
- sociodrama—the enactment of social roles;
- psychodrama—the drama of the psyche.

Moreno sees the philosophical "universals" as spontaneity, creativity, time, space, reality, cosmos and Godhead, that underpin life and therefore influence the philosophy of his work. Here, I focus on spontaneity and creativity and Moreno's understanding of their place in human experience. Moreno sees spontaneity as the primary source of creative energy in the universe manifested in each individual. Spontaneity can only exist in a universe that is not determined by absolute laws, and where some degree of novelty is continuously possible, so leading to creativity. Here, I describe how it is manifest in infant development, role theory, mental well-being, tele, sociometry, and sociograms. I then discuss their place in the methodology, my role as researcher, metaphor, and the right and left brain.

Infant development

Moreno watched spontaneity in children at play, uncluttered by expectations, in free authentic living. Moreno perceived play as spontaneous social enquiry central to the integration of creative/scientific research and therefore at the heart of his existential philosophy (Moreno & Moreno, 1994). Moreno saw children as spontaneous creators in developing relationships through play, while Montessori (1963) was to describe children's activity as spontaneous enquiry; that of learning how to order their environment as scientists. Jennings was later to describe this paradigm in developmental terms as "Embodiment (touching body); Projection (playing with toys) and finally Role-play (interacting with others)" (Jennings, 1992, p. 14). Professor Robert Winston in *Child of our Time* (BBC 1, 22 May 2008) argues for the importance of play to mental health and education. Play facilitates relationship interaction. Play leads to infant psychic understanding that emerges through embodiment (taking experiences in), projection (putting feelings out) and role play (being able to sense or understand the experience of the other as well as the self) (Jennings, 1992, p. 14). This infant development Moreno represents in the psychodramatic methods of doubling (embodiment), mirroring (projective play) and role reversal (role-play).

Psychoanalytic theory reflects this triadic frame with the stages of the omnipotent position (I rule the world); the paranoid–schizoid position (I should rule the world) and the depressive position (I have to share the world). These positions dovetail with Freud's stages of psychosexual development. Freud saw babies as being born with energy or psychic energy that he called libido. This energy had to be organized by the development of a well-tuned mind. The energy of the libido was irrepressible, like spontaneity. The libido was focused on searching for gratification through different psychosexual stages: oral, anal, phallic, latent, and genital development that affected the attitude towards life.

Moreno saw these three stages as the psychosomatic roles, the psychodramatic roles, and the social roles (see "Role theory", below). Whatever theoretical model is pursued, these stages or positions continue to be worked on throughout life in our interactions (play) and negotiations. Thus, warming up to *play* is at the heart of spontaneity.

Role theory

The beginning of role theory in reference to modern psychotherapy and behavioural and social sciences is often attributed to Moreno (1934) but Mead (1934), and Linton (1936) also contributed to the theory of roles. However, in the early 1800s, Reil (1957) recognized the therapeutic significance of mental patients acting out interpersonal difficulties.

Moreno's principles of role theory are the central psychological and relational evolutions that emerge from spontaneity. The role is created by past experiences and the cultural patterns of the society in which the individual lives. Every role is a fusion of private and collective elements (Moreno, in Fox, 1987, p. 62) Moreno made a combination of theatrical form with the metaphor of daily life.

> We thus define the role as the functioning form the individual assumes in the specific situation in which other persons or objects are involved. The symbolic representation of this functioning form, perceived by the individual and others is called the role. The form is created by past experiences and the cultural patterns of the society in which the individual lives, and may be satisfied by the specific type of his productivity. Every role is a fusion of private and collective elements. Every role has two sides, a private and a collective side. [*ibid*.]

Moreno, like Hume (1777), holds the view that roles do not emerge from the self, but, rather, the self emerges from the roles. True to his immense capacity to draw on different resources, Moreno was inspired by Democritus (*ca* 460–370 BC), who, all that time ago, envisaged the theory of the atom opening up the modern conception of the universe. At that time, it was seen as the primary unit. Moreno wanted to describe the smallest unit of human relationship as social atoms. This influenced his theory of roles. This is also a Buddhist perception from some 2,500 years earlier. Moreno perceives three categories of roles:

- the psychosomatic roles: the walker, the sleeper, the eater and other body roles;
- the psychodramatic roles: their experience of their mother, their teacher, their daughter, internalised or fantasy roles—the social atom;

- the sociodramatic roles: the mother, the teacher, or daughter— the social, real or cultural roles.

They tend to develop in this order. No role can function without corresponding roles. You cannot be a sibling on your own; a mother does not exist without a child; a teacher without a pupil; a political activist without a government. These relationships of two belong to clusters of relationships, such as the group of the family, creating a complexity of experience between the family members as well as within each one of them. Roles are, therefore, both external and internal clusters. Holmes (1992, p. 40) describes the formation of these clusters as a process of association in the psyche, or a clustering of object relationships forming in the infant's mind. These internal clusters, whether you call them roles, social atoms, or object relations, influence the infant's response to the world and, thereby, the world's response to the infant. Thus, the theory of roles mirrors the Copernican revolution in human knowledge articulated by Kant (1781) and Hume (1751). They see that it is not only the mind that conforms to things, but that things conform to the mind. Role theory is the relational context to the theory of spontaneity.

Spontaneity and mental well-being

Moreno observes that, although spontaneity is not tangible, it is an observable phenomenon through body, facial expression, and behaviour. Kipper (1986, p. 11) understands spontaneity as "a form of 'energy', it is not a concrete substance. So the immediate moment is seen as the most important and psychologically the most meaningful time unit". This idea is not unique. Other philosophers, such as Descartes (1637), Kant (1781) and Hegel (1807) recognize that intuition precedes empirical knowledge. Intuition is the place where the knowledge of human experience begins, "freed of everyday impressions" (Descartes, 1977, p. 22). Intuition is at the heart of spontaneity.

Moreno holds that spontaneity and mental well-being go hand in hand. To take the implications of this further, mental health is manifest in the capacity for spontaneity that, in turn, is rooted in the present moment. This is because it is the only moment that can be changed, and it is, therefore, pivotal to creativity. Thought and feeling about the past can be changed, but the past itself cannot. Likewise, expectations of the future are influenced by a sense of self in the present. Hence, each time we step out of the present we are out of the moment of spontaneity, losing our response to the here and now and the empowerment of creativity. When we lose our flow, it is usually due to some aspect of anxiety that creates a stiffness and is in opposite polarity to spontaneity. Spontaneity rises and falls like the waves of the sea. In spontaneity there is flow, adaptability, integrity, creativity, and mindfulness. It involves the whole person. It is to be separated from mindlessness or impulsiveness. Spontaneity is a source of creative energy expressing a new response to an old situation or an adequate response to a new situation (a true reflection of how the person feels and thinks). This creative act contains an element of surprise made manifest as phenomena of human behaviour through concepts Moreno devised called tele, sociometry, and sociograms.

Tele

Spontaneity possesses a quality that Moreno observes as something prior to and beyond the given reality. This remarkable quality he calls tele. Tele is attraction, indifference, or repulsion between people. "Individuals have a certain sensitivity for each other" (Moreno, 1934, p. 157). This sensitivity is over distance; it is not fixed or permanent, but elastic in all relationships. To understand tele, Moreno takes us back all the way to Thales of Miletus, in 585 BC, who identified an attractive power in ferrous materials that had more than one chemical. Then, two thousand years later, Mesmer (1734–1815), possibly influenced by Mead (1673–1754), thought this attractive power was within and between animal bodies. Moreno called this attraction tele, and describes this disance effect of a socio-physiological mechanism. Tele expresses the simplest unit of unconscious feeling transmitted from one individual to another.

Think of times when you are in a new group and someone has to be chosen for a task. It might be you or someone else, but you know or sense who it will be. You do not know why, but then find out you are right. This is a truly wonderful quality deep inside you.

It has relatives in intuition, imagination, and empathy in closer relationships, but none of these manifests knowledge at a distance in the way that tele does. It is my experience that, however unwell a person is, tele is always accessible. It takes them by surprise. Tele is impermeable, so it is also a reassuring healthy role that can encourage confidence and contribute to a recovery of well-being and mental health. Tele influences conscious and unconscious relationship choices and, therefore, influences the pattern of roles between and within people. It is expressed in sociometry.

Sociometry

Sociometry is a method for mapping relationships according to significant criteria. Sociometry unfolds and measures the myriad of networks, different size constellations, and durations of fluid social interactions like a geography of a community. These maps are built upon significant choices to the group. Who do I turn to for advice? Who do I choose as leader for the group? Who do I want to live with?

> Sociometry is a manifestation of the spirit of democracy, a humanistic approach in which people are recognized as being creatively involved in their sociological process and should not be thought of as mere organisms on whom scientists do research. [Blatner & Blatner, 1988, p. 137]

Moreno sums up sociometry as "a qualitative structure integrated with quantitative operations; it acts from within" (Moreno, 1934, p. 23). Here, again, the basis of sociometric classification is not the psyche that is bound up with an individual's organism, but individual organisms moving around in space in relation to other things and other organisms also moving around them in space like stars in the sky. Moreno devises a simple technique for recording sociometry, called sociograms, that capture relationships between people.

Sociograms

In its time, Moreno noted that the "sociogram", or chart, of sociometry was a new form of map, if not the only form of structural analysis of a community (Fox, 1987). Moreno (1934) like Pierce (1934), takes pragmatic democratic processes as the source of problem solving. Williams captures their approach in a delightfully down-to-earth description: "People are unendingly curious about where they stand with others, pecking orders, heart to hearts, alliances . . . and consequently gossip. In other words they are informal sociometrists" (Williams, 1991, p. 127).

Sociometry has been widely used by sociologists, anthropologists, and economists, but has been less evident in psychotherapy. Sociometry is a tool of great simplicity, fluidity, and clarity, rooted in the here and now. I find it indispensable to my practice, and hence the research. Moreno's design of sociometry is a science with the purpose of transcending and achieving the potential in all human groups: to love, share, and face truth. He summarizes the spirit of this endeavour in a sweeping, perceptive statement: "If the nineteenth century looked for the lowest common denominator of mankind, the 'unconscious', the twentieth century rediscovered its highest common denominator—spontaneity and creativity" (Moreno, 1934, p. 20).

In the research, I intended to use sociometry not for the purpose of mapping the intricacies of an ongoing group, but as the principal technique by which to record how the opposite sex twins negotiate between themselves and the other members of the group. The purpose is to mark communications as expressions of relationship experiences of opposite sex twins. In this way, I intended to reflect the complexity of experience that emerges between conscious and unconscious knowledge that can be expressed through tele. Therefore, I used the sociometric principle of what happens "between" the opposite sex twins as the point of focus to assist my task: that of illuminating the phenomena of opposite sex twin relationship experiences.

Methodology

The structures that illuminate spontaneity in the research have been described as tele, social atoms, and sociometry. These emerge among the European philosophical phenomenologists, Husserl (1931) and Heidegger (1977), who sought the underlying structures of experience, the essences or defining elements, without which the phenomenon would not be what it is but another phenomenon (when, where, who, what—time, space, reality, and the self). Phenomenology was noted in Kant's writings as long ago as 1765, but it was Hegel who came to elucidate it further. Hegel (1807) held that knowledge, as it appeared to consciousness through perception and the senses, led to an unfolding of the consciousness of experience as phenomena through which science and philosophy could move towards absolute knowledge. For Descartes, Kant, and Husserl, knowledge based on intuition and essence preceded empirical knowledge.

The principle of spontaneity is validated through the rigour of transcendental phenomenological methodology (TPM), designed by Husserl, who held that "ultimately, all genuine, and in particular, all scientific knowledge rests on inner evidence" (Husserl, 1970, p. 61). Moustakas endorsed this methodology: "What we know from internal perception can be counted on as a basis for scientific knowledge" (1994, p. 45). The reader interested in methodology is referred to the website www.hiddentwins.com.

My role as researcher

My intention was to find some way to research and communicate in a form as near as possible to my practice as a psychodrama psychotherapist, through spontaneity. Spontaneity, I came to understand during the research, is influenced by my abilities and disabilities. Spontaneity reflects aspects of my personal life in which art, sculpture, and dance embody metaphor that bridges the gap between the unspoken, or unspeakable, and the spoken and written word. I use to think these non-verbal forms of communication were my attempt to muffle a gap made wide by my "shameful stupidity" as a dyslexic. So, for the research, I had to turn this disability around into an asset. I was going to have to find a way to use words with spontaneity and a spring in my step. I tried poetry. I found it easy to write but tiring to read. Try again. I conceptualized physical activity and visual images for the collection of data. This was easy. It did not primarily involve words. But for the communication of reflection, I would need words. To produce this book, I would need to find a way to move from the concrete to the conceptual. I then conceived the whole research as a musical sculpture that required a literary medium. Every group of words was a sound in my head, so a sense of music and song reverberated into sound sculptures of words that I, as researcher–practitioner became a conductor, could conceive of as solos, duets, trios, and chorus. I conducted, and was being conducted by, the sounds and silences in the rigour of spontaneity, creativity, embodiment, and metaphor. I had a research plan, but there was no rehearsal. I followed the music of spontaneity that ebbed and flowed with the energy and buoyancy of the research group; the playfulness and spontaneity within the structured activities, painting and talking, that balanced with the chasm of the unknown. Braud and Anderson (1998) state that where there is truth, there is a concert of many voices; where there is such a concert, or symphonic agreement of voices, there is power. My strategy to keep my spontaneity vibrant through the metaphor of action, art, and reflection was mirrored by Braud and Anderson. I was encouraged. I then discovered, to my surprise, that Transcendental Phenomenological Methodology follows the same process that I had made as a dyslexic, moving from the concrete to the concept. So, with this surprise in my pocket, I could turn to what was most familiar in my practice, the use of spontaneity, creativity, and metaphor, to illuminate what was hidden and forbidden in the relationship experiences of opposite sex twins.

Metaphor

In my practice and, therefore, in the research, I tend to see relational representation, however ordinary, as metaphoric. Thus, different forms of metaphor are integral to the research as modes of expression. Metaphor makes a place to play in the mind. It is verbal sculpture. The outcome of the collection of these "metaphors" might lead to a synthesis in the research design illuminating emotional meaning heard in the duet music "between-the-twins".

Right and left brain

The very process of this book has been a synthesis of the "opposite sex twins" of right and left brain, through Moreno's philosophy of spontaneity and phenomenology. The splitting of the scientist–explorer of the world without from the artist–expresser of the world within is an impoverishment of the mind. It is exciting that contemporary research is now redeveloping integration between the sciences and the arts. Psychodrama is primarily action-based (right brain), while Transcendental Phenomenological Methodology is primarily word-based (left brain). I experience them as complementing and challenging each other. Likewise, the split between Western and Eastern psychology and psychotherapy is beginning to dissolve. Western philosophy tends to be rooted in individualism, while Eastern psychology tends to be rooted in the group. Western psychotherapy is increasingly aware that to neglect the place of the group within the psyche of the individual is to neglect a doorway to knowledge.

Following the phenomenological principle of synthesis, I had taken up a new academic mantle as researcher–practitioner that has paradoxically increased my creativity. There is here a synthesis of academic–creative twin in which the resonances between the research methodologies have invigorated each other. Abraham (1999) puts this in another way when she speaks of the perfect platonic union of opposites upon which the successful outcome of the opus depends. This is not sexual; it is opposite-sex twin. I have come to see, with excitement, the immense value of researching through spontaneity, tele, and sociometry. They are phenomenological handmaidens to creativity, curiosity, and enquiry, insight and surprise. Through these, this book is not a definitive textbook, but a tapestry of experiential fragments that sets out to illuminate the relationships of the social and private roles of opposite sex twins, expressing their lived experiences, informing social and professional practice, and reflecting on human experience. With this in mind, my research design is described in the next chapter, Chapter Four.

The research design

SEBASTIAN: . . . yet thus far I will boldly publish her: she bore
a mind that envy could not but call fair . . .

(Shakespeare, *Twelfth Night*, 1601, 11.1: 29–30)

F ollowing on from the theoretical underpinning of spontaneity,
this chapter presents the research design. I show how I organized the different levels of activity to warm up the group of
opposite sex twins to themselves and each other by moving from
representations of their external roles to their internal roles through
representation of themselves as individuals, as twins, and as
members of the group. Data was collected from activities and paintings in Workshop I. There were questionnaires at the beginning and
end of the research, providing a private expression through words.
These, with their comments on Workshop 1 (Chapter Five) and their
reflections in Workshop 2 (Chapter Six), provided the verbal data to
the research.

The design had three stages: the individual interviews, the pilot
study, and the main project of Workshop 1 and Workshop 2. There
was a year between the pilot study and the main project of Workshop
1. The Workshops took place approximately six months apart.

The individual interviews

The interview design involved their family stories, sociograms, paintings, and comments. I conducted an individual all-day interview with each of the opposite sex twins in the following stages.

- The family stories (Chapter Seven) gave context to the opposite sex twins' experiences.
- The sociograms, maps of their world, were made by the opposite sex twins from objects available in the room. These they chose to represent significant persons and ideas in their lives.
- They commented on their sociogram.
- They role reversed with any of the significant figures they chose in their sociogram, to gain further insight into their own understanding.
- The paintings were made on A3 size paper. Ten coloured paints and brushes of varying sizes were laid out randomly. They painted three pictures, one of which was painted blindfolded or with eyes closed, the second was with the left hand, and the third was with the right hand. The theme was "how they feel as a twin". Each of these paintings was made in less than five minutes. They then reflected on their three paintings. They consented to the transcriptions from the individual interviews being included in the book.

The pilot study

I used the material from one set of opposite sex twins, Diana and Dan, in order to test how I could use the methods of painting and sociograms as data collection in themselves to compare with the data collection from the comments the opposite sex twins made at the time (Figure 5).

In studying the sociograms, I listed the similar and different positions of the objects representing significant roles and compared these to those in the sociogram of the other twin. I noted that this showed a surprising number of similarities, for example:

The paintings

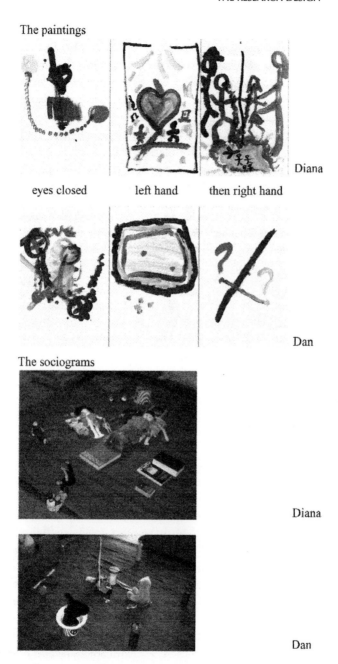

Figure 5.   The paintings and sociograms from the pilot study.
See also the colour illustration between pages 158 and 159.

- where they positioned themselves in their map;
- their lovers at their feet;
- their twin and family behind them over a shoulder, the opposite shoulder;
- the absence of father in their original sociogram.

With the paintings, I noted the colours, shapes and size of brush strokes made by each twin (Figure 6). The aim was to look at similarities and differences, and to avoid making interpretations as far as possible. However, there were striking similarities, for example:

- the overall shape of the blindfolded painting;
- the square shapes in the painting made with the left hand;
- the line down the middle of the painting made with the right hand;
- the similarity of colour use when they had ten colours to choose from.

I then highlighted the similar and dissimilar themes in the comments of these opposite sex twins. However, as can be seen in Figure 7, the outcome of their *comments* showed more differences than similarities, while the sociograms and paintings showed far more similarities than differences. I was not sure if this was due to the lack of rigour applied to collecting the themes from the "word texts" or whether it was reflecting the difference between conscious and unconscious communication. It was, therefore, important that the data collection of the "word text" in the main project was challenged by the rigour of the phenomenological methodology employed in this research (see www.hiddentwins.com).

With this proviso, I decided to use the principles of action, blindfolded painting, and the comments of the opposite sex twins in the main project of Workshop 1, and the resources of reflection in Workshop 2.

The sociograms from the individual interviews of the other two pairs of adult opposite sex twins can be seen on www.hidden twins.org

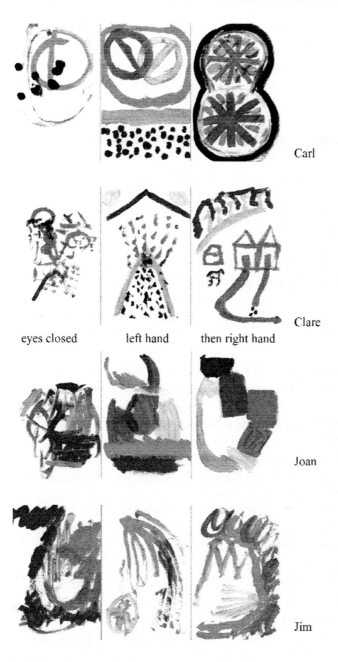

Figure 6. The paintings from the other individual interviews.
See also the colour illustration between pages 158 and 159.

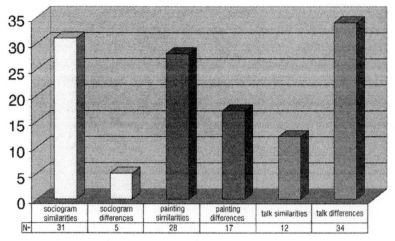

Figure 7. The findings from the pilot study: similarities and differences between one pair of opposite sex twins.

The main project

The main project involved all three pairs of opposite sex twins. The research design of Workshop 1, the action workshop, consisted of sociometry and psychodramatic activities, their paintings, and their comments. The workshop engaged the opposite sex twins in a range of activities, to which they had agreed. This was filmed and edited.

Paintings were made at the beginning and end of the day. Each of these twelve paintings took them no more than five minutes.

- They were blindfolded or with eyes closed, as they painted on A3 paper.
- They had six colours laid out in the same order, and a variety of brushes.
- The theme was "how they feel at the time".
- They did not see these paintings until Workshop 2.

Workshop 1

The arch of the action in Workshop 1 was designed to create a warm-up to a rise and eventual decline of a wave of spontaneity. To create this, all the activities were short, light, and designed to develop safety in the group to allow each individual to gradually become more spontaneous, to go into their own experience, and then to share with the group through their body language, words, and silence. This warm-up to intimacy reached its deepest level in the early afternoon in Workshop 1 through the single gender groups. The result of the activity was a spontaneous consolidation of observations made by the opposite sex twins during the different parts of the day. Workshop 1 started with boundaries.

Action 1. Boundaries

A discussion was initiated on the issues of boundaries and confidentiality similar to all groups, but I added the following for this particular group.

- What the twin knows that the group does not know.
- What can be said to the group but not to their twin.
- What they know about each other's spouses.

Action 2. Painting

They were asked to paint, blindfolded or with eyes closed, how they felt at the start of the day as described above. These were not seen until Workshop 2. See website www.hiddentwins.com

Action 3. Sociometry

Sociometry is the pattern-making of their social relationships. Sociometry was achieved here by the opposite sex twins positioning themselves in relation to a central point in the room according to how they felt towards each named relationship experience with, for example, their father, mother, siblings, self, children, twinship. The group could choose the relationships about which they were most curious and, therefore, were most important to them.

The main outcomes that surprised them were:

- they were more interested in what their twin did than what they did themselves;

- they were faced with their own contradictions;
- the scores from the sociometric choices were surprisingly similar;
- their relationship experiences were curiously distant.

Action 4. Warming up to each other through a series of tasks

- *Tele.* They were asked to imagine about each other's profession. This was a way of getting to know each other individually in the group and exploring their tele and intuition about each other. Their capacity to perceive what others did for a living, they thought, was surprisingly accurate.
- Pairing activities
- They paired with their twin and reflected on their birth order.
- They paired with others as if they were twins.
- They tested the distance they felt to another group member of the opposite sex and then to their own twin.
- They shared, through mime, the most important feeling in their relationships.
- They shared the second feeling that arose for them in relationships through allowing other members of the group they chose to represent their two feelings that could accompany or conflict with each other.

Their comments on these activities raised themes that surprised them. Here, and throughout the book, words in italics indicate those chosen by the opposite sex twins. These became part of the language of this research.

The main recurring themes were:

- something *reciprocal, a resonance,* in the twin pairings;
- *brutality* is the experience of feeling sidelined by their twin;
- feelings that also arise with opposite sex twin relationship experience are those of generosity and confusion; generosity *vs.* brutality; trust, security, and, by the same token, lack of trust and insecurity;
- *all kids physically fight,* although they did not fight each other;
- they feel *shoved together/pulled apart* in different social and internal ways.
- *surprising patterns of performance;*

- one of each group pairing and one of each birth twin pair wanted feedback from the group while the other did not;
- half the group did not want to know or say. This meant one of each twin pair withheld. One pair had not wanted to share the first feeling but wondered how they would fit in. They also did not share a second feeling, or expressed a reluctance to see their withdrawal expressed by the group;
- curiously, unless they were paired with someone, their observations of feelings expressed by others in the group were not as accurate as their observation of professional roles.

A lunch break was taken in the kitchen. This was a social event. They talked as a group, in small groups, and in pairs. This was not included as part of the data, as it was not recorded.

Action 5. The separate gender groups

After lunch was the most radical moment in Workshop 1, and possibly the first time that opposite sex twins had gathered together in groups of their own gender. Their choice of topic was the most urgent question for them, and they chose "how are their romantic relationships affected by being an opposite sex twin?" Their comments raised themes that were ordinary, surprising, and puzzling.

Ordinary themes

- Extra pressure on the family; for example, they could not share clothes.
- They were not sure of the impact on other siblings and tended to demonize them.
- It was *easy for them to meet up with the opposite sex* through the friends of their opposite sex twin.
- The opposite sex was *ordinary, not remote and exciting.*
- They did not feel *opposite enough* for the second stage of relationships.

Surprising themes

- They felt *marginal.*
- The *architecture of their psyche* was different.

- They *saw themselves as a pair.*
- They *knew things about each other that the family do not know.*
- *Although they hoped not, they felt affected by their twin.*
- *They did not feel differentiated enough,* so they needed a *Darwinian* explanation of how to survive. They had to learn to be single. Attempts to separate resulted in *see-sawing or flip-flopping;* holding an opposite feeling to the other twin.
- *They did not feel sufficiently male or female,* or fascinated by the opposite sex, as they were so familiar to them.
- *They were equals* because they were the same age.
- *They tended to choose inappropriate partners.*
- Incest was not significant except when stirred by distance.
- For support, the women looked to their twin. The men looked elsewhere.

Puzzling themes

- If they had met opposite sex twins before they had not realized it.
- They found that others felt like them. This gave them autonomy.

Action 6. Group sculpts

Towards the end of the workshop, each member of the group was invited to sculpt their experience of being in the group. Their comments showed that none of them liked where their twin in the group had placed them in the sculpts.

Action 7. Painting

Painting, with their eyes closed, how they felt at the end of the day. These were not seen until Workshop 2, along with film from Workshop 1 and the sociograms and paintings from the individual interviews that preceded the workshops. The colour illustrations of the sociograms and paintings can be seen on www.hiddentwins. com

The next layer of data, from the dialogues of the thoughts and comments by these opposite sex twins about what they did in Workshop 1, are set out in Chapter Five. Workshop 2 is fully described in Chapter Six. It took place six months after Workshop 1. It was the reflection workshop in which the opposite sex twins saw the film made of Workshop 1. They then looked at the creative work of the paintings from Workshop 1, and the sociograms and paintings from the individual interviews. Consent forms were completed by the opposite sex twins for each stage of the research and book.

CHAPTER FIVE

Comments by the opposite sex twins during Workshop 1

SEBASTIAN: . . . My bosom is full of kindness, and I am yet so near the manners of my mother that upon the least occasion more mine eyes will tell tales of me.

(Shakespeare, *Twelfth Night,* 1601, 11.1: 33–36)

Their comments as immediate responses

During Workshop 1, at the end of each section of activity, the opposite sex twins had stopped or sat down to comment on their experience. Their immediate responses were recorded and became part of the verbal data of the research. This chapter sets out the comments of these opposite sex twins. These immediate comments should not be confused with their reflections in Workshop 2 (Chapter Six), which took place six months later and were, therefore, not their immediate responses.

The opposite sex twins commented that some of the activities led to encounters that were "ordinary" to anyone's relationships; some left them "puzzled" as to whether others felt the same as they did.

Other activities "surprised" them. For example, they had not recognized before that there could be experiences common to them all *because* they were opposite sex twins. Their comments are presented within the seven action stages laid out in Chapter Four.

Action 1. Ordinary and puzzling issues of boundaries

All therapy groups start with the issues of boundaries, confidentiality and expectations. This group was no different. Joan said, *We each of us can decide what we want to say and what we can't.*

There are groups involving family, friends, and colleagues similar to this group, but it was surprising to the group that the hidden knowledge and fantasies in these relationships was so clearly expressed.

Jim said, *There may be quite intimate things in twin relationships vs. spouse relationships which may be quite sensitive with the other twin and their spouse.*

There was another unusual and surprising negotiation about membership to this group; Dan offered, *If my twin wants to say something and doesn't want me to hear I can go in the garden.* Diana, Dan's twin, was silent in response to this attempt to problem solve a shared space. There was intimacy and willingness to be present, even through making themselves absent. I had never heard of confidentiality being handled in these ways. Was it peculiar to the unusual situation of the research, where the opposite sex twins could think about their relationships as opposite sex twins with their twin? This, after all, was something none of the research group or I had ever experienced; the possibility of learning to manage rivalry, love, and discernment in the self with their opposite sex twin as well as with other relationship experiences.

The expectations the opposite sex twins had in relation to participating in the research also reflected the uncertainty and novelty of engaging in it. Carl wanted to explore similarities and differences of experience that other twins have. Clare *did not want to feel odd.* Joan wanted to discover whether the relationship *changed for the better* or worsened as they aged. Jim wanted to *reflect on (the self) as an individual.* Diana wanted to *spend time with her twin,* which in itself was rare. Dan wanted to share problems and strategies, to see if they find the same *tensions, resentments, emotions.*

Action 2. The morning paintings

Reflections on all the paintings are discussed in Chapter Six.

Action 3. The sociometric graph of choices

The sociometric graph recorded the relationship patterns around significant relationships (Figure 8).

The opposite sex twins chose relationships that mattered to them. These were listed down the left hand side of the graph. Surprisingly, a high percentage of relationships were distant. This sociometric activity at the start of the day gave the group a way to get to know each other and how they were alike and different in their relationship choices. Their questions asked were followed by their answers. The order of questions have been summed up below and have, as far as possible, followed Workshop 1.

Close to venue	C	C	C	C	D	D
Relevance of the research	C	C	A	D	D	D
Relationship world	C	C	C	A	D	D
Relationship to twinship	A	A	D	D	D	D
Same sex relationship	C	C	C	C	A	D
Partners	A	A	A	A	D	D
Children	C	C	A	A	A	A
Authority figures	A	A	A	A	D	D
Mother	C	C	A	A	A	D
Father	A	A	A	A	D	D
Past	A	A	D	D	D	D
Present	C	A	A	A	D	D
Future	C	D	D	D	D	D
Self	A	A	D	D	D	D
Happy being twins	C	C	C	D	D	D
Prefer to be a same sex twin	A	A	D	D	D	D
Prefer to be an identical twin	A	D	D	D	D	D
Life influenced by opposite sex twinship	C	D	D	D	D	D
Answers based on 1st 16 years	C	D	D	D	D	D
Siblings	A	A	A	A	D	D
Choose not to be a twin	C	D	D	D	D	D

Scores : 21 Choices

Key of choices

C = Close   - 24

A = Ambivalent - 48

D = Distant   - 62

Figure 8.   The sociometric graph.

How relevant was the research to their lives?

In each twin pair, one twin appeared to feel the importance of the research while the other appeared not to. Carl, the older twin, felt the relevance of the research to his everyday life, while Clare felt distant from it. Joan, the older twin, felt distant from the relevance of the research, her relationship world, and her twinship. In contrast, Jim felt close to the relevance of the research and to his relationship world. Diana, the older twin, felt her twinship and relationships were important to her, so the research was relevant. In contrast, Dan did not think the research was relevant to his every-day life, although relationships mattered to him.

Were their answers based on how they felt in the moment?

While the past for the opposite sex twins was difficult, their present lives were comparatively good, although their futures were less sure. None the less, following the philosophy of the importance of the present moment and spontaneity, they were asked to give answers about how they felt at the time. During the sociometry, all the opposite sex twins were able to do this except Dan, whose answers were *predicated on the first 16 years of his life*. This greatly annoyed his twin, who felt the research was invalidated. They both said that if they had made their choices from the other time zone, their answers would be entirely different. There was a sense of mayhem, of being pulled in two directions, that also threatened the validity of the research. Like a mother with opposite sex twins, I had to find a middle ground that validated each twin. We could go no further until I suggested that we often had feelings from the past, or about the future, in the present that affected how we lived in the present. In this sense, the past and future were part of the present moment. This was accepted as a phenomenon they recog-nized. It seemed to contain the anxiety that difference was disas-trous and would lead to too wide a gap for an encounter between these opposite sex twins. It had also challenged the philosophy of the research based in the spontaneity of the present moment. No present moment is pure, hanging in space without a past or future.

The next activities warmed them up to being together through different pairings and as a group, which facilitated encounters between them and raised different relationship issues.

Action 4. Pairing with their twin. How important is birth order?

This small group of opposite sex twins were all born 7–10 minutes apart. Carl, the first-born, said, *As the first, I don't remember it,* while Clare thought, *As the second I preferred to be the youngest and thereby the youngest in the family.* However they both thought if they had been in the other birth role, *It would make no difference.* Joan, as the first-born, said, *I felt no responsibility. It was an accident of birth,* while Jim said, *As the second, I feel abandonment.* They both thought that to be the first gave confidence. Diana, the first-born, felt *Blamed and insecure; as the second I would be more protected and secure,* while Dan felt, *As the second, bloody well last in line again, but compensated as the only boy, and, having an opposite sex twin as a sister, we were not compared.* But Dan also thought if he had been the first, *It would not have made any difference.*

Hence, two of the opposite sex twin men preferred to be first-born, while the third, who was first-born, saw no significance. In contrast, two of the women preferred to be second-born and the third, a first-born, imagined she would be less confident if she was second. Confidence and responsibility belonged to the first-born, while protection and security was seen to belong to the second-born. The birth order also illustrated the cultural status of males over females. The male preferred to compete with a male rather than a female.

Did all children fight to find out their place with their
siblings and peers?

Fighting, for the opposite sex twins, had a variety of expressions described in the following dialogue:

Carl: *We took on weaker people!*
Clare: *Big brother used to whack us. I didn't take a pop at him, he was too strong!*
Joan: *I don't remember fighting other girls and boys. My twin brother fought the younger sibling and I was the alleged peace-maker. I suppose that role was my fighting.*
Jim: *We demonized the younger brother.*

They also took opposite positions about fighting.

Diana: *I didn't . . . fight my twin brother—he was way too strong for me.*
Dan: *I was always lost . . . you used to taunt me for being such a weak-ling!*
Diana: *I remember physical fighting amongst all the siblings in my family.*
Dan: *Were you in the same family?*

Did they feel pushed and pulled, shoved together or kept apart?

This was part of a discussion that took place in response to their activities around their important feelings in relationships.

Joan: *I can't remember feeling pushed together but Jim clearly did.*
Jim: *It's not social. There is a more fundamental level of no differenti-ation beyond the fact that one happens to be a man and one female. You have got two choices. Either being wide apart or very close, and what you really need is to be sufficiently differentiated to be able to relate successfully at the appropriate distance.*

Diana thought she must keep a distance from Dan, Not because of incest but because he is the only boy. Dan did not respond to this but said, *At the younger age you are shoved together with your twin. Even if we didn't get into the same class you finish the school day together. We had a core of different friends, different activities, the same as every-one else.*

Did they value same sex relationships?

Carl, Joan, and Diana, the oldest in their twinships, all said they valued same sex relationships, while their twins, Clare, Jim, and Dan, were not so sure.

When they worked in different pairs did they tend to twin in those pairs?

Bion and Foulkes (1985) saw coupling between people as a form of defence against the task. This coupling, pairing, or twinning may be true here, but there may be other meanings that are reflected upon in Chapter Eight. Examples of these couplings were seen in the activity of sharing of feelings important to them in relationships. Clare paired with Dan.

Dan: *The two emotions . . . which we didn't want to share.*
Clare: *So how do we get around that?*

Dan also paired with Joan, while Jim tried to pair with Diana.

In the closure of Workshop 1, Carl paired with Diana. Wistfully, they expressed a wish for a continued shared space together as a group and with their own twin.

Diana: *Are we going to go on forever?*
Carl: *Every five years!*

How did their twinship affect their relationships?

Carl, Clare, Joan, and Diana were happy being opposite sex twins and preferred to be opposite sex twins. Joan felt that her twinship had little influence on her life. Jim said he not happy at being any sort of twin, *and would prefer not to be a twin.* Dan felt *ambivalent* about being an opposite sex twin. This was a curious contradiction, as Jim talked far more about being a twin than his twin sister. These contradictions seemed to capture a duet that resonated and hovered in the space between the twins; Jim called it *see-sawing,* in which perceptions represented opposite thought positions. This way, they could look individuated. That was to say that, while they tried to individuate, they were in fact maintaining their twin duet by appearing to hold the opposite position to their twin. They wondered what this did to their other relationships when their primary relationship was one of an oscillating see-saw duet. How did this affect their intimate relationships?

How did they express feelings in Workshop 1?

Carl, apparently the quieter of the two, expressed two feelings important for him in relationships: *kindness and insecurity.* Clare found it hard to share with the group about her feelings but, later, in the absence of Carl in Workshop 2, she reflected, *I can't remember what I was hiding. Nothing nuclear!* She then expressed herself through him.

It's not that he wouldn't want to be here; he would not be able to face it.
It's to do with revealing his innermost . . . Actually he's the same as me,
it nearly killed me so I understand it totally.

In the expression of feelings, Joan and Jim had a different response. Joan initiated by sharing her feelings of *patience* and *tolerance*. Jim described her as *Confused underneath, manifested as being bossy*. She tried to explain, and Diana tried to rescue her, by saying her *Eyes were darting—self conscious, not quite secure*. After this, Joan did not share her feelings, while Jim expressed his two feelings of *Trust and security, lack of trust and insecurity*; and *extreme fear and anger*. He wanted six feelings expressed. Joan, his twin, perceived these as *frustration* in him, while he was perceived by Diana to express *generosity*. This could be seen as a reversal; Joan tried to express patience while Jim was seen to express generosity. These reversals were also seen in the matching of the paintings and sociograms in Chapter Six. Again, this was not peculiar to relationships, but, for these twins, it also could express some of the complexity of how they were seen and how they felt. Again, nothing unusual in this, as couples often are misread, but unusual because the couple of twins is so primitive, as will be discussed in Chapters Nine, Ten, and Eleven.

Diana tried to portray *Kindness, generosity*. She was perceived *as caring, nurturing*. She wanted *brutality* represented in contrast to kindness, while Dan said he did not want to declare his feelings but he was happy to have feedback. Dan's actions were seen as *Power and control*. But Diana perceived Dan's action as *suffering—a pissed offness*.

This was not the only time that the twin's perception of their twin was not the same as that of the others. Was she protecting him or simply knew him more deeply? Whichever, Diana perceived and named feelings in others, but Dan continued to make no comment.

Hence, the attempt to individuate and the fear of offending were upheld.

Was there a difference of attitude between the twins?

Opposite attitudes were held about the interpretation of their actions as *resonant*. Resonance between the pairings was understood by Clare, Jim, Carl, and Diana.

Diana: *Both of them were quizzical. We both had the same one* [movement]. [They were alike] *in their physical actions. So if I had been twinned with you* (pointing to another member of the group) *it would have been a different one, and reciprocal.* Dan took a different position, *You've added one and one and come up with three. It was fortuitous.* He turned to his then group partner, Joan, who gave him her support.

This dissonance also demonstrated the position so often taken between the twins that was far more familiar to them, as is often the case between siblings and other couples.

Action 5. Discussions in their same sex groups

These groups raised issues that could be familiar to anyone but had special meaning to this group of opposite sex adult twins as they explored who they were and what they were about.

What did they think of being their own sex?

Carl: *I can watch rugby. I know all about it . . . but it doesn't move me.*

Jim: *Men, in our society, are expected to have a male identity which is manifested in a strongly developed life story.*

Dan: *There is a blokey context which we don't know about, not that I want to sit and discuss shoes.*

Diana: *We have no girliness. I am built feminine but I can remember thinking when girls were being girly-girly, how pathetic. It was in order to revere men and for men to love women! I remember pretending to be girly!*

What did they think of the opposite sex?

Clare: *Some women aren't girly but seem to be deferential to men. Does this wonderful man exist anywhere? We always knew that it wasn't true. That's why we got a proper job!*

Joan: *I remember being struck by the normality of accepting all the things to do with boys in our house. We simply didn't have to bother.*

Jim: *The opposite sex twin is just ordinary to us and not ever so remote and interesting and exciting as they may be to singleton boys growing up. But the corollary of that is that it is difficult to progress from having a girl as a friend to having a girl as a girl-friend; that it is easy to get into the intimate situation but then what, because you are not opposite enough.*

Diana: *Female opposite sex twins don't see men as dominant, other than maybe physically, or idealize them. They see the weaker side. We are always used to having a male there, absolutely contemporary. When I was younger . . . we were all just the same and now I think . . . phew, we come from a different planet.*

Dan: *At school other boys were round the back of the bike shed getting all excited when they discovered what a bra looked like. I had to battle through them to get to the bathroom! It was not a great achievement! It reminds me of the movie,* What Women Want. *To a certain extent, because I have a twin sister, I could tell what they were thinking about, what they liked, what they didn't like. So you could relate but, by God, doing anything with that information was useless! We had all the advantages and we blew it!*

What did they think about their relationships with husbands, wives, and partners?

Joan: *Four of the six are not married. Half of us don't have children. It would be interesting to compare this with other twins in similar circumstances.*

Jim: *I am the only one who's living full-time with a partner!*

Carl: *I find it difficult—its killing, intimating my deepest thoughts that I think about in the middle of the night, so if you . . .*

Clare: *My partner is sort of part-time. I've had crap partners. I am crap. I think I was frightened of the commitment.*

Diana: *We both pick inappropriate partners! I've sort of given up. Girl-friends are the relationships I am most close to. There has been a conscious effort on my part to become more secure as an individual.*

Dan: *I've not had many intimate friends. Such friends have usually been in other parts of the world. My closest intimate friend is my flat-mate. At work I'm closest to my female colleagues. I do not relate well to men in a non-sexual way.*

For security to whom did they turn?

For security the women turned to their twin. The men turned to other women or friends.

Carl: *I find it difficult to share intimate stuff . . . I mean sometimes you think you're different, but maybe that's the way a lot of people are.*

Clare: *I get security from my twin brother and from my friends, from my job, and other members of my family, not my older brother . . . Carl and I get on very well.*

For security Joan turned to her husband and her female friends, while Jim turned to his wife. Diana and Dan chose different people.

Diana: *In a crisis my twin brother would be the person I would tell.*

Dan: *In a crisis I would tell my flat-mate and my work colleagues.*

Action 6. How did the sociometry of sculpting the group contribute?

Through the sculpts of the group, they were invited to sculpt or place themselves in the group as they had experienced it at the end of Workshop 1. Carl arranged the group in a circle and slipped himself in the middle, saying, *I don't know what I'm doing here. Right, all come in. I'll stand in the middle and I'll rotate like that restaurant, this way and that.* Clare responded that she did not think about it.

Clare placed the women opposite their twin, but in a circle, with *The men further from the women, on purpose.* Carl called it, *Like a rugby scrum.*

Joan and Jim did not like the position given them by their twin's sculpt. Joan's sculpt placed her twin next to her with the group in a horseshoe in front of her with herself in the middle. Jim said, *I feel too close to my twin.* Jim then placed the group in front of him with his twin hidden at the back. Joan said, *I'm quite resigned, I have to peep through here.* Jim's response was, *There was some brutality there. I've got into serious difficulties, giving the contradictory messages (very close/very distant) to people.*

Diana made a circle, women opposite their twin, like Clare's sculpt. Dan said, *You put us against our own twin.* Dan then placed his twin at a distance, to his left, behind others. He then made a horseshoe, like Joan's sculpt, with himself in the middle, and put his twin in front of him but outside the horseshoe. Diana said,

I found that very brutal, in front of everybody, for my opposite twin to put me the furthest away. On seeing the film, Diana then reflected, *My interpretation of my twin's position for me was not what he meant. Almost, it was the opposite.*

None of them liked where their twin placed them in the group sculpts. It was through this that *brutality* in their opposite sex twin-ship was expressed by this group.

Moments' play between their opposite sex twins

Joan moved towards Jim, her twin, who reciprocated by moving away. She had another attempt at trying to link with Jim. Joan said, *My twin and I are the ones with pieces of paper and a pencil. Married people make lists!* (they were the only married twins). Jim replied, *Management consultants have clip-boards!* Again, Jim expressed his discomfort at being close to his twin, as he was in her sculpt group.

An expression of playing was between Diana and Dan over chocolate cupcakes: this could be between any two people, but it was unusual for these opposite sex twins to have fun together. As Diana expressed at the start of the day, it was unusual for them to spend time together.

Diana protested to Jim, *You can't go straight from sheep to humans' sexual behaviour . . .*

Dan joined in the fray;

Dan: *She has taken refuge in the chocolate!*
Diana: *At this point!* (laughs)
Dan: *Nothing else left.*
Diana: *Nothing else left, no, no!*
Dan: *Other than Cadbury's Dairy Milk . . .*

Action 7. The end of the day painting (see Chapter Six)

There were anomalies that enriched the tapestry of opposite sex twin encounters that showed:

Difficulty in seeing and hearing in the sculpts

Diana: *I can see the action, I can't hear what is being said.*
Dan: *Can I ask what is the difference of her position? I cannot see.*

Was there a role of castration or sexual suppression?

Jim and Joan: *In agriculture, when you are breeding sheep, you get the teaser ram, who by vasectomy, is set to run with the ewes for two weeks before the real ram is introduced, so they'll do the business.*

This story may be a metaphor for the experience of opposite sex twins. Were they the teaser ram to each other or to the public? Were they the ewes? Were they both? The literature suggested their sexual desire for each other was expressed in their intimate relationships, but Jim thought *the problem with opposite sex twins is that they suppress each other's sexuality. What each twin may need is a teaser from outside the twin pair to trigger their sexual responses appropriately.*

Was sexuality influenced by being an opposite sex twin?

Diana: *I feel like I make men gay. They only had another child because they wanted a boy, who then turns out to be gay!*

Dan: *I can remember specific comments . . . on my lack of masculinity. I concede* [it] *had no effect on me. Was I gay because I've got three sisters or I've got an opposite sex twin?*

These questions raised more questions. Did being an opposite sex twin have some effect on being gay? Anecdotally, I have encountered a surprising number of opposite sex twin men who were gay, but only one opposite sex twin female who was gay but said she adored her twin brother. Could there be a connection to the research on the shift of hormones in the womb? Neuroscience has linked body experience to brain development. Furthermore, does this link also work in reverse? Does imagination know something we cannot see? Could it be that Diana's imaginings are true that she made her twin gay, or simply an attempt to keep her special twin relationship with her twin brother because she felt they were kept at a distance, or both?

This chapter has described resonant and dissonant fragments that reflected the rich variety of feelings, thoughts, and encounters between the opposite sex twins, sometimes playing, often opposite and see-sawing. The outcome is at times clear and at others jumbled, confusing, and unresolved. These were glimpses of bubbles magnifying and diminishing the impact of each other, creating a mobile dialectic pattern of opposite sex twin relationship experience, rather than a position of individuals. When this mobile pattern was held at a distance it created a frisson of energy, sizzling, soothing, defying, challenging, laughing, withdrawing, but never ever separate, whichever way they are looked at. It was a unique sort of individualism, peculiar to all twins, but with the glamour of being an opposite sex twinship that also brought with it the ensuing bleakness of intimate relationships, as Jim described,

> *The idea of always having someone else there . . . from the womb, seeing yourself as part of a pair. It is not to do with an individual that is my twin. It's to do with the architecture of the relationship. The world actually doesn't run like that, you have got to change . . . because it is not set up for pairs!*

> *If you are a twin you have already got your other half, it feels, everyday, so the whole idea of romantic love doesn't work for me! That's another factor that puts you in the sort of marginal position. Thinking of yourself as an "us" the whole time is not sustainable. When that breaks up (when a twin's marriage breaks up) there is a kind of Darwinian issue; how are you going to survive? The answer is that you have to learn to be a singleton, you have to adapt. As twins grow up, they are aware of the need to differentiate but can't, and the way they do it is, if they see one being happy, they say I'll be sad. If they see one being angry, they say I'll be nice; so you learn see-sawing. That's a real problem when you are living in an adult relationship.*

The architecture of opposite sex twins' sense of being, their psyche, their twinship, and their individuality were not constructed with the same design as that of a single child. There was a poverty in their sense of place manifested in their relationships. How things appeared was not how it felt. In Workshop 2, the reflections by these opposite sex twins on what they said and did in Workshop 1, while looking at the film, gave further insight into their understanding of their experience.

CHAPTER SIX

Workshop 2. The opposite sex twins' reflections on Workshop 1 and the individual interviews

ANTONIO: Have you made division of yourself
An apple cleft in two is not more twin
Than these two creatures. Which one is Sebastian?
OLIVIA: Most Wonderful!

(Shakespeare, *Twelfth Night*, 1601, 5.1: 231–234)

Workshop 2, like the individual interviews and Workshop 1, was scheduled for the duration of a whole day. Workshop 2 was originally designed, for ethical reasons, for the opposite sex twins to validate the film made in Workshop 1. But it became much more. The opposite sex twins wanted to reflect on the paintings and sociograms as well. I was ready to stop this exploration at any point when their energy flagged, but the opposite sex twins became intrigued by the tasks, as will be seen in their reflections. This enabled the opposite sex twins to respond spontaneously.

In this workshop, the reflections of the opposite sex twins on the film, the paintings, and sociograms were tape-recorded and transcribed. These transcriptions became part of the verbal data of the research, and the opposite sex twins gave consent for them to be included in this study. How the film, paintings, and sociograms were looked at by the opposite sex twins is set out below to give context to their reflections that follow.

Looking at the film

The forty-five minute film was constructed with separate sections for each activity.

- A menu bar facilitated finding a particular section of the film.
- The group of opposite sex twins watched the film together.
- At the end of each section the film was stopped for the group's reflections.
- They reflected together on the film as a whole.

Looking at the paintings

Stage 1

- I laid on the floor the six paintings they had done blindfolded in *the morning* of Workshop 1. Each was number coded.
- The opposite sex twins looked at the paintings and the task was for each of them to see if they could pair the paintings visually based on their own choice of criteria, and then to write down the pairings by the codes. So each person in the group had noted down three sets of paired paintings.
- This was repeated for the blindfolded paintings they had done in *the afternoon* of Workshop 1.
- They shared their findings with each other and discussed on what criteria they had based the pairings.
- They then looked at the six morning paintings and the six afternoon paintings again, and the pairings they had done for the morning and the afternoon, and were asked to see if they could match the morning ones with the afternoon ones pair for pair.
- They shared their findings with each other and discussed on what they had based the pairings.

Stage 2

- I laid out the eighteen paintings from the individual inter-views. There were three for each of the twins (blindfolded, right hand, left hand), all number coded. This was eighteen months after they were originally done, so, although it was not the task to identify again their own, some did say later that they had forgotten which was theirs.
- They were not asked to put these paintings into groups of which they thought were done with blindfold, left or right hand. They were asked to categorize them visually into six groups of three paintings by their own criteria, writing down the codes.
- Then they were asked to see if they could then pair each group of three paintings with another three.
- They shared their findings with each other and discussed on what criteria they had based the pairings.

Looking at the sociograms

- The photographs of the six sociograms were laid on the floor. These were number coded.
- Transparent photographs of the six sociograms were also provided.
- The opposite sex twins were invited to look at and then twin the six sociograms into three pairs.
- The opposite sex twins could lay one photograph upon another to think about their criteria for the pairing of the sociograms.
- They recorded their pairing of the six sociograms on paper by number code.
- They discussed their choices and the criteria by which they reached them.

(See the sociograms from the individual interviews on the website: www.hiddentwins.com.)

The process by which the film, paintings and sociograms were organized was to facilitate their reflection as a part of the validation of the research methods so that the outcome of meaning was enriched. Action, paintings, and sociograms, all non-verbal methods of communication, challenged each other as well as the verbal communications of these opposite sex twins. Their reflections on these methods of communication are organized below. The chapter then closes with the twins' reflections on the impact of the research experience as a whole.

Their reflections on seeing the activities in the film of Workshop 1

The extracts were written in fifteen dramatic scripts as sequences of moments or scenes to preserve the spontaneity and to illuminate the relationship experience of these opposite sex twins. On seeing the film the opposite sex twins were surprised that many of their choices and thoughts had not changed during the gap of six months between Workshop 1 and Workshop 2. As this surprised them it was held to be significant. Carl found *the film at times hilarious and at times excruciating to watch.* The film was how they expected it to be.

Their reflections on seeing the sociometry

Carl, Joan, Jim, and Diana were happy with their choices, and did not want to change anything. They did not know if they would be happy with it in the future. They still felt the same; they were not surprised. However, they had further reflections.

Joan: *I am surprised that the women are incredibly consistent and the men aren't.*

Jim found the sociometric methods, *Very powerful. I'm aware of the subterranean things beyond articulation of words that can be a smoke screen. The stuff underneath is expressed more when you are moving in physical juxtapositions. This may have been the first opportunity to express how I feel. It is not the sort of thing that you can express in any other situation. Body language–physical juxtapositions!*

Their reflections on seeing other activities

They found that the different activities produced different responses in them.

Diana: *When we made our choice about being with a same sex twin, in the sociometry, I did not want to be with a female twin then. But I had a different response standing with another female twin, thinking, it might not be that bad. That is exactly the point of doing these different ways; to see what happens as responses can be different in different activities.*

Joan also found being with a same sex twin *feels very comfortable.*

Their reflections on being with other opposite sex twins in the research

Diana: *It enables me to understand that I am not alone and other females of an opposite sex twin feel like me.*

Jim: *It reveals things about me and my twin that I had not thought about.*

Dan: *Let me put it more crudely, are we, my twin and I, as screwed up as I think we are in our relationship? Or are the rest of you also as equally screwed up in your relationship? I'm delighted to say we are pretty much on a par!*

Their reflections on being with their twin in the research

Carl: *My twin and I seem to mirror each other's behaviour and gesture. There is a degree of tension bubbling beneath the surface.*

Joan: *There is something there that is too difficult and touchy to integrate.*

Jim: *It must be worse than just judgemental; Nuclear options!*

Diana: *My choice of distance to my twin isn't how I feel about twinship, it is how I feel about our relationship . . . standing closer wouldn't necessarily mean that we are in a good relationship. By standing at a distance it doesn't necessarily mean that we are in a bad relationship, but that we are distant from one another.*

Dan: *We see the same event so differently.*

Their reflections that some twins shared while their twin remains silent

Diana: *I still can't understand the reluctance to just say what it was you are feeling. I was upset. It is almost worse not to know.*

Dan: *A lot of these exercises are inviting me to throw the nuclear option. We could have wrecked the whole proceedings. On the one occasion when I did do what I chose I got what I expected back; you got upset.*

It seems that those who speak get thought about and those who listen feel guilty.

Joan: *My twin learnt that I am totally ignorant of how he feels. Should I feel ashamed? My lack of empathy maybe?*
Jim: *My twin learnt more about how I have responded to the dilemmas of being a twin, in comparison with how she responds.*

These reflections are enriched by their discussions on the paintings and sociograms.

Their reflections on the paintings

Figures 9 and 10 show the twins' morning and afternoon paintings from Workshop 1.

Their reflections on the process of painting selection

(See the paintings from the individual interviews on the website: www.hiddentwins.com)

Dan: *I did the boring ones first.*
Clare: *I think I did crap.*
Dan: *I'm sceptical. It is bewildering . . . I didn't even recognize my own paintings!*
Diana: *I can't do it* [as] *separate people, I've got to do couples first and then split it up* [to decide who did which painting].

Their reflections on how they paired the paintings
through differences

Dan: *I think that if you are to put a different combination of these paintings together with no name of who has done them you would be able to find similarities!*

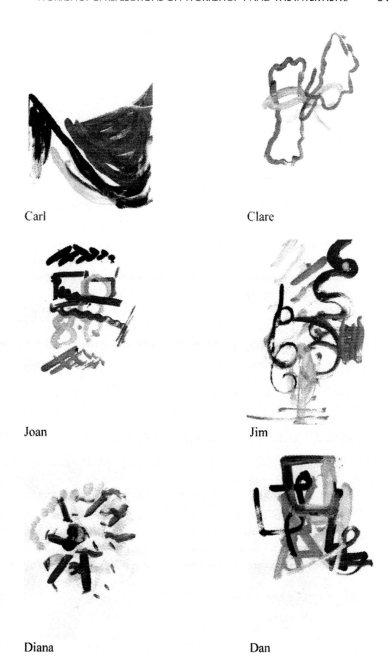

Carl   Clare

Joan   Jim

Diana   Dan

Figure 9.   Their morning paintings (with eyes closed) from Workshop 1.
See also the colour illustration between pages 158 and 159.

Figure 10.   Their afternoon paintings (with eyes closed) from Workshop 1.
See also the colour illustration between pages 158 and 159.

Diana: *I am saying you are doing the opposite of what you are saying!* [trying to choose by opposites but in fact choosing by similarities].

Their reflections of how they paired the paintings through similarities (see Figures 9 and 10)

The opposite sex twins find they select on grounds of shape, brush stroke and colour in the paintings.

Jim: *If we try to group them into a group of three, you can tell that these are all in the same group, and those are all in the same group, and these are all in the same group.*

Joan: *Curiously, they do kind of match!*

Diana: *In fact, the couples have all painted the same; those two are squiggles, those two have got some symmetry, Dan has got a square I've got a circle! They paint the same! Most of the paintings are in two halves.*

Jim: *This one is done in outlines and this one filling in.*

Dan: *One is carefully and gently shaped, the other is aggressively painted.*

Jim: *They are complementary in different ways. You can get different examples of the way they work together.*

Diana: *How can those two paintings both do spots? How could they both do black spots?*

Diana: *I would say that those two in particular are by the same person, and I'd say those two are the same person, and those two are the same person.* [In each case the paintings were done by a pair of twins.]

Clare: *I guarantee that the same person did those two.* [They were made by twins.]

Diana: *This is odd, That is amazing! Those six which are so obviously together. I just think those are so alike. Mind you, so are Dan's and mine, and look at those—Joan and Jim. They have got the same style with similar shape. They don't look exactly the same but they kind of fit in.*

Jim: *They are complementary. If you use just half of them, if you divided them, they would only be half. They need each other.*

Dan: *I accept the premise that there is likely to be a similarity certainly within the artist and probably within the grouping of the family. What I am saying is you're making a leap further.*

Joan: *Lots of colours going backwards and forwards, Which way round? It doesn't make a lot of difference really. That is the way it is. The colours are touching each other which denotes a certain closeness. There is a sort of balancing act. I think the one done with my eyes shut demonstrates an interlocking of space, the intertwining of the twin relationship.*

Diana: *Symmetry, those two are really big heart, big square. That just kills me, that one mirrors the other one. They are an algorithm, a mathematical model from the relationships between the colours and shapes. Would a mathematician come up with a closer correlation than if you put six paintings together randomly? What I reckon is that the scores would be similar for each of the couples, so that Dan could be shown that, measured on these indices. I mean, to get two people on different occasions to paint these two paintings and come up with such similar things is extraordinary, isn't it? Just looking at it, you can say these are about 8% similar. And the question is, so what? What does that mean, how do you value that? It is fascinating that the twin should paint the same. I don't know if brothers and sisters paint the same. But, first of all, before you go any further, you have got to prove that the style is the same. Do it through digital technology!*

The sociograms. How they paired them through similarity
(See the six pairs of sociograms in www.hiddentwins.com)

The opposite sex twins matched the sociograms to see if the different medium of relationship maps produces different strategies of matching and different reflections. They chose by group shapes, objects, and space. When examining these sociograms, the opposite sex twins were provided with transparent photographs so that they could lay one transparency over the other to see what happened. The photographs were not always a perfect fit so this limited the method, but they were accurate enough to illuminate the perceptions of the opposite sex twins in terms of complementarity, similarity, and difference. The sociograms were numbered for matching by the opposite sex twins. After their private reflections they discussed their findings.

How they found the process of putting the sociograms into pairs

Jim: *I got them all completely wrong except my own.*

Joan: *I got them all wrong as well except my own!*

Dan: *I knew which one was mine, so working on Diana's theory of similarity and opposites, I knew hers. But, against myself, I can analyse those two and those two, but I couldn't analyse those two. They had to go together by process of elimination. I can't work out why they go together. So then it was just a question of working out which two were together, bearing in mind we had seen the paintings.*

The sociograms of Carl and Clare

Dan: *I'm assuming that's yours?* [to Clare] *Those two have to be the same. Sporadic, special, no great mess.*

Diana: *It's not scattered like the others.*

Jim: *To me it is very interesting but there are those figures all along there in Clare's story, and in Carl's story, on the top. They're sort of side by side. I mean it literally completes the picture for me.*

The sociograms of Joan and Jim

Dan: *I would imagine that is Jim and that's you, Joan.*

Jim: *The other way round.*

Dan: *I should have really thought about it. Yours, Joan, is more ordered.*

Diana: *Based on my theory of similarities, and overall pattern the only thing I can see is that they are both scattered. There is a style of similarity.*

Clare: *Like a mirror image.*

Jim: *I relate this to my feelings that there is a space that can only be occupied by the other person. I describe it like a chemical valancy; you've got a space that you need someone to complete.*

But there were also differences;

Joan: *This one has a centre but doesn't have a bottom. This one has got a bottom.*

The sociograms of Diana and Dan

Dan: *That was mine, that looks like Diana.*

Diana: *You can see now, that Dan and I put ourselves in the middle of the teddies and the layout of the whole shapes. I still think the twins are doing similar things.*

Jim: *That's like what happened with the painting. This one has got a crowd here and that one has got a crowd there.*

Clare: *So it is like a mirror image.*

Diana: *There is a style of similarity. I think they are very similar.*

Their reflections on the content of their own sociograms

There were responses to looking at their sociograms again ("you" refers to the researcher).

Clare's sociogram

Clare: *All I remember is putting my older brother against a cushion because he was a rag doll and would fall over, and you said he couldn't stand on his own two feet!*

Researcher: *The only person sitting up is Mother, the teddy bear, and she is off the mat.*

Clare: *Ah, that's because she lost her whack!*

Researcher: *Carl's sociogram has everybody, including Clare, the doll bottom right, except the seal representing Carl who is lying down or without a body.*

Diana's sociogram

Diana: *Gosh. Did I tell about the doll in the middle? Then like Dan all the men are on their backs in pain. And the most terrible thing happened. I was completely traumatized. This was Daddy, the lion, that I put in and she said "What can daddy see that you can't see?" So I looked at the doll. It is a two-sided doll. I lifted up the doll's dress and it was a two sided doll, on the other side of the doll was a wolf! Red Riding Hood and the wolf! That was weird.*

My observations as researcher on the sociograms

- The objects used by the women tended to be lying down.
- The women tended to show closer relationships than the men by the arrangements of the objects being closer together.
- The women chose larger objects than the men.
- The women placed themselves close to their twin brother but turned from him.
- The objects used by the men tended to be erect.
- The men showed one intense relationship to the exclusion or avoidance of all others.
- The men portrayed their twin sister as a small object behind them.

The sociograms, in spite of these differences, showed unexpected similarities of relationship pattern or fitting together of these patterns that had been apparent in their activity in Workshop 1 and their paintings. The opposite sex twins added significant reflections and understanding to their relationship experiences in their comments and reflections on their activities, paintings, and sociograms. These comments and reflections validated the research methods in Workshop 1 and are summed up in their closing reflections.

Unknown to the opposite sex twins, their reflections of the twinning of the paintings and the sociograms were surprisingly similar to my own in the pilot study. In the sociograms, they saw the overall similarity or complementarity of shape. In the paintings, they had used colour, shape, and brush stroke to choose which painting to twin with which.

Their closing reflections on the whole research experience

Carl: *It made me reassess my life as a twin. Twinship is special. I feel more unique. We feel even closer.*

Clare: *Being a twin is quite different and affects many areas and decisions in life. We are not closer. Others are closer.*

Joan: *There is more "same-ness" than I had ever imagined—that was a revelation! His perception of me was not at all what I had thought. It has revealed things about me and my twin that I had not known/thought about before. It's a unique relationship and has tremendous effect on life decisions and affects relationships with mates in later life. My perception of my place in the family was not what I had thought up to now.*

Jim: *Meeting the others confirmed my struggle to develop a quasi-singleton identity. The night after the last group meeting I slept right through the night for the first time in ages—a very remarkable reaction. Unfortunately, it hasn't been sustained.*

Diana: *It enabled me to understand that I was not alone and other females of an opposite sex twin feel like me. Being a twin is significant and affects relationship with mates in later life.*

Dan: *It gave me insight into past incidents. We both saw same incidents so differently. She was much more affected than me. We seem to be closer.*

Joan: *It is extraordinarily rare to get three pairs of opposite sex twins together. All that we did made us think about things that maybe we had not thought about before, ever, or maybe we had not thought about for a very long time, so you were bringing up to the surface emotions and thoughts about relationships, all sorts of relationships, not just the twin relationships that we maybe had not considered before. So the corollary from that is that maybe there were things that were introduced and discussed that were very hurtful to one or other of the twins.*

Jim: *I have spent a lot of my life searching for answers. I felt very alone and couldn't find answers. The idea of all being in the same boat is extremely important.*

Diana: *Are we going to go on forever, a twin commune, seeing as we are all barely married?*

Jim reported that he had one night where he slept the entire night through, while Joan, who had not been able to absorb milk as an infant, brought everyone Welsh cheese in Workshop 2!

My reflections as researcher on Workshop 2

The main project was designed to this small group of opposite sex twins, from different communicative standpoints: through their eyes, hands, voice, body, and interactions; through their feelings, imagination, intuition, and thought. This multi-storey design was like a perspex three-dimensional noughts and crosses, in which relationships could be seen vertically and horizontally at the same time so each dimension of the research could be used to mirror a reflection, a misfit or a contradiction, and thus illuminate the relationship subject. This conception was endorsed by the Communicube, invented by John Casson (1998); ". . . a transparent, open, five level structure" that enables people to explore aspects of self, their relationships with others and their view of the world.

In my quest to make a coherent whole, I orchestrated particular themes to give an arch of the unfolding experience for the opposite sex twins during the research, through the non-verbal experience, the verbal experience, the reflection experience. These particular activity tools illustrated the relationship experiences of the opposite sex twins through the principles of spontaneity and creativity, described in Chapter Three. The aim was to discover what was missing and how this could be seen, felt, and described in the here and now.

The workshops and interviews seemed to be containers, like a playpen or a playground. The catastrophic terror of murder or death of the self and/or twin was contained by these frameworks. While these opposite sex twins came together to help with the research, their own reasons percolated through. By the end, Dan told me that I was *irrelevant*. I was delighted and rejected. Perhaps this was Mother's feeling. They, on the other hand, had a greater sense of themselves as opposite sex twins and, therefore, as individuals. This outcome brought me back to the importance of play. I recalled Moreno watching children in the park and the principal phenomenological philosophy of the research, spontaneity. Through "playing" with action, painting, and discussion, these opposite sex twins found they could interact and share what felt to them the unique feelings of being an opposite sex twin more freely. The outcome was set against the background to this research that would contextualize and challenge the foreground of it. The background, described in the following chapter, Chapter Seven, is the stories of their families told through the words of these opposite sex twins.

The family stories told by the opposite sex twins

SEBASTIAN: (to Viola, disguised in her brother's clothes)
Do I stand there? I never had a brother:
Nor can there be deity in my nature,
Of here and everywhere. I had a sister, . . .

(Shakespeare, *Twelfth Night*, 1601, 5.1: 235–238)

T his hilarious scene encapsulates family strife and trickery that quicken our listening to the family stories told by these opposite sex twins. In this chapter, I have described the social roles of their families and how the opposite sex twins felt about them. The stories were taken from the individual interviews at the start of the research. I selected relationship headings, apparent in all the stories, that involved grandparents, parents, migration, siblings, favourite, health, professions, and their opposite sex twin relationship. These three families worked to better themselves from harder times. The recurring themes added a historical/socio-economic context to the research. Further reflection on the context of the families was beyond the scope of this book. The introductory summary is a weather eye to the rich story telling that followed.

Although edited and sequenced, the stories have remained in the words of these opposite sex twins.

The introductory summary

The grandparents

The role of the grandparents had a powerful influence on the parents, and consequently their grandchildren, especially in terms of the roles of men and women. There was:

- a grandfather in the ministry with a wife who frequently took to her bed;
- a grandfather who was a fine jeweller and philanderer with a wife who gave birth to eight children and died early in poverty;
- a grandfather who was an entrepreneurial gypsy with a wife who tolerated her husband's over-close relationship with their daughter.

Migration

The parents of each family migrated in pursuit of economic betterment.

- From the UK to New Zealand.
- From the city to the country.
- From one city to another.

The professions of the parents

The professions of the parents were seen as respectable and valuable to their community.

- Chicken farming. They also had horses.
- Fruit tree farming.
- Medicine and law. They also had horses.

The families all lived in big draughty houses.

The parents

The status of men and women was similar to the generation before them.

- The husbands were seen to marry above their station, while the wives were seen to marry down.
- The fathers were absent, angry, hardworking, and entertaining.
- The fathers were more important, but the mothers tended to be cleverer, creative, and hardworking.
- The mothers were unhappy, depressed, breaking down, or suicidal.

The resemblance of these opposite sex twins to their parents

- Carl and Clare perceived themselves to be like their parent of opposite sex in looks and personality.
- Joan saw her role as head girl to be like that of her mother.
- Jim, like his father, was extremely angry and undervalued.
- Diana took up the career her father wished to do himself.
- Dan thought he was like his father except that he is gay.
- The opposite sex twin females did not want to be like their mothers.

The siblings

Troubles in the twinship did not exclude troubles for and between other siblings that were not discussed in this research.

- The twins could be a hitting board for older siblings.
- The twins could be a fighting battalion against younger siblings.

The favourite

- The opposite sex twin men, Carl, Jim, and Dan, were favourite, the sick twin, the first son and heir, or the only son. They put no store by this, even though one recognized he was closest to mother.
- The opposite sex twin women related to mother but did not feel close to her.
- The opposite sex female twins tended to feel close to father, kept their distance from mother, or found a substitute or sibling.

Their health

- They reported good physical health.
- Two of the twins nearly died from digestive problems in infancy.
- Three of the six twins had psychotherapy.

Their professions

The opposite sex twins worked in people-orientated business: organizational management, media, childcare, bed and breakfast, teaching, dentistry, gardening, building.

The opposite sex twin relationships

- These opposite sex twins got little TLC and touch.
- There was polarity in what the twins knew and what the family knew.
- There was a tendency for a twin to pair with another member of the family rather than their twin.

Competition between the opposite sex twins

- The male opposite sex twins did not see the females as competition.
- The female opposite sex twins felt equal to the opposite sex.
- The female opposite sex twins worked hard for their place in the family.
- There was covert fighting. The opposite sex twin females fought their twin by mediation, withdrawal, siding with an older sibling, or getting their father's approval (and money).
- The opposite sex twin males fought their twin by withdrawal or humour.

The story of their family told by Carl and Clare

Their maternal grandparents

Carl: *My maternal grandfather was very keen to go to Presbyterian church in the Wirral. He was born in 1888. The family was religious and there is a long line of missionaries, three of whom were doctors in India, Thailand, and New Zealand. Mum had two sisters and a brother. I think my Mother is Welsh. The grandmother was a difficult person. Perhaps it was because my Dad took her daughter when she was young. Grandma had two speeds; one was slow and the other was stop. She had always been the poorly one and took to her bed for a long time, ever since Dad first met her in 1946.*

Their Dad's family

Carl: *My Dad was born in 1920. Dad has got two brothers; Charlie used to build houses and Bob worked for an American engineering company.*

Their parent's meeting

Carl: *My parents met at agricultural college. My Mum was very creative and sporty. Dad was an ex war veteran . . . and fought in Africa. He was looked up to at college. He was probably drawn to her shy smile, blue eyes, and they got along. When they took their exams she passed. He ended up with qualifications [now] called NVQs.*

Clare: *My parents are so different as people. If you think of Mum, you are thinking of sort of artistic type. Dad, you are thinking of down to earth, very nice jokey kind of life and soul of the party, like Carl. He was very good at being outward, gregarious, and not so good at telling you his innermost thoughts. Dad was an anchor. He wasn't particularly religious. They were very proper. I believe Mum married beneath herself. Her family were furious with her. Her family stayed in the Wirral, the better place. We used to go to church because Mum loved singing.*

Their brother, his family, and their maternal grandmother

Carl: *My brother qualified as a vet and now works in the poultry business in New Zealand. He doesn't communicate much. He was treated harshly by my father in some respects. He is not very close to us twins but has kept reasonable contact with our parents and is closer to Rosemary, our elder sister. My brother [also] married someone working on the poultry-training course in 1979 in the Wirral. His son probably takes after his father, always been easy and trying to do the right thing. His daughter is exactly like her maternal grandmother.*

Their older sibling sister

Carl: I would say Rosemary, our eldest sister, and Clare were more like Father, but he didn't like to play favourite. It's just that us boys got a heavier time from him.

Clare: At a very young age, of about sort of five, I took the lead from Rosemary because Mum was airy-fairy.

Mum's breakdown

Carl: Mum and Dad had rows. It was difficult when us twins were born, especially for her, with her mother dying, but they got through. Mum had a fiery temper. She'd get fixed on things . . . tunnel vision . . . she would get angry if you didn't do what she wanted to do. Mum did start to drink alcohol at one point in the late 1960s. It was quite a long trip to the hospital. There was electric treatment. She walked off, got out of there. Dad picked her up. The marriage was pretty rocky at that point. Mum was less unhappy pursuing her interests, painting, singing, and writing. I, as a young baby, was quite sickly because I refused to eat food . . . I was saved by a doctor. I was eleven months old.

Clare: There was no support for Mum at all. They moved to this place in the country that had a small farm and it was quite a distance from the town. She put us to bed in the afternoon and cycled off two or three miles and left us completely and utterly on our own. Could you believe this! She just left us, we would not dream of doing this now. I said it was illegal. She said what else could I have done? So we then moved. We didn't have a lot of money. I have no children but I have had abortions, so I have had the opportunity but have decided to have no children. I am not the right person. At the back of my mind is it from her? My Mum didn't have her own source of money.

   She works very well; she is a very intelligent woman. My mother had a mental breakdown. They gave ECT in mental *hospitals. It was the New Zealand fashion. I mean, she wasn't that loopy. It's just not really much support from the husband who would have no idea how to help. He did his work, that was his support. I mean, I have a memory from a very young age of her tying my shoelaces and me thinking she is not there in her head. Mum obviously was having some sort of crisis when she said she didn't like the clock ticking; and if you have anything you want to complain about, write it down. The good doctor was away and the bad doctor sent her straight into hospital. The good doctor came back from holiday and told her to get work. That's what she wanted to do, so then she went off to start to train in Wellington. All this time I am pissed off because I have got to do all the cooking. The breakdown was when I'm 9–13. You can't play with your friends after school and have to come and peel the spuds.*

I do remember that when Mum got a job at the boys' school and she dressed in a mini-suit and drove by I was proud of my working Mother for some reason. She was proud of herself. Dad liked her working. Most women didn't work. It was sometimes looked down on. Mind you, she had been with us until we were nine and we were thirteen when she started. She was obviously outwardly happier but I didn't want to grow up that quickly. I didn't want to do that work [laughs]. I didn't want to do all that cooking, you know, and I am sure it had a bearing on my choice not to marry and have kids.

The horses

Carl: *I would be there sort of helping and grooming the horses, playing around. I didn't feel as if I was left out.*

Clare: *Dad was very keen on horses. Carl hated riding. Mum hated horses. I rode because I knew you had to, although it was quite a good thing to do as everybody was doing it. For Dad, I think this was aspiring to class.*

School

Carl: *I always remember clinging to the steering wheel so I wouldn't be able to go, I was so unhappy. I didn't have any problems there, it was just the separation.*

Clare: *We didn't want to go to school at all when we were five. Later, we went our own ways; I went into science and he went into arts, so there was no competition.*

Who was favourite?

Carl: *Clare might tell you that I was Mum's favourite. I don't think it was that significant. I'm thinking of a baby photograph in which they couldn't get me to smile and Clare was the jolly, smiling one. I'm not saying that I'm necessarily an anxious person ... But I don't feel that I'll have a breakdown. I can usually get on with people. I can grow things and cook things and make things. I'm not good at talking about myself. I tend to shy away and go sideways and never talk about myself. Mum would have been closest to me because I was sick at an early age and she felt protective towards me. I don't know if Clare resents it or not. I know the relationship is close now. She rings up every week. Clare can be quite an anxious person. The more I see this the more I go the other way. She is aware that she can get anxious. She can be a steadying influence when I get anxious. I'm always criticizing what I do.*

Clare: *Mum has always felt worried about Carl. Carl nearly died when he was a baby. When I was young I had jet-black hair and Carl was totally Mum and I am totally Dad. So we can't be from the same genes. He's like Mum in personality as well and I'm like Dad. He is more forgetful, I am totally much more ordered. I've seen it in same sex twins. Girls. It's like sometimes one twin is white and one is black. It is kind of strange. You've got polarization.*

Being opposite sex twins

Carl: *There was one imaginary friend called Mari McLaine who we used to play with. And we used to chase around the place a deformed rooster who used to chase us. I still feel there was something around the two of us. There's a sort of your own world, your understanding, the way you see things. It's hard to describe something that's there [laughs] it's not as if you have known anything different. Blue is my favourite colour and she wears red a lot. When I am anxious I feel pink.*

Being an opposite sex twin means that you are different from the rest of this world because there are twins out there but most of your growing up period you identify yourselves . . . you are always known as the twins like a label, so that label is not an individual but a group of two people. Being boy–girl twins you're not probably seen the same. The rest of the world doesn't see it quite the same as maybe you see you. The idea of two people and you have your own role, and then there is a barrier between you and the rest of the world.

It's more relating to pre-school, you know, you had your imaginary friends. We used to play and we were kind of isolated in the country so we didn't tend to interact a lot with other people. If Clare likes or dislikes the other person [I am going out with] *it can influence me.*

Clare: *We all feel responsible for Carl, or do I feel more responsible because I am his twin? The thing I have been trying to escape from and haven't at all is responsibility. Dad is very close but he isn't that close to Carl. He is quite critical of Carl. If I speak to Dad of what Carl is up to, I make it sound a lot better than it is, so that he won't worry. I've only got Dad's approval because I have worked for it. Mum has always felt worried about Carl. Carl nearly died when he was a baby. So that part of you, that maternal instinct part of you is put to one side or locked away. Of all the things that affected my childhood I would imagine I have always thought Mum's breakdown was probably the biggest when she came out. Her memory had completely gone. She didn't recognize people. That just shocked me. Never was I told you should get married, and certainly I was told to go to university, get a good career.*

Being an opposite sex twin is a bit like a volcano, on the one hand it is explosion and it is also calm, but you get on better with that twin than you ever would with another brother or sister. Is it because you are with that person, you are the same age, you play with that person far more because you are the same age, you are developing at the same stage, or is it because you are genetically or not genetically more similar? I think it is probably because the advantages of being a boy–girl twin to me were having a friend of the opposite sex of the same age. I would much rather be a boy–girl twin than a single sex twin because of the advantages during the school years and afterwards. Carl and I had imaginary people that we played with, which Mum used to, of course, go completely along with, because she is a bit bizarre anyway.

You can never escape from being a twin, you couldn't escape if you wanted to. The weirdness of living on a volcano. I have always thought I would rather be a twin than not be a twin. I'm protecting him. He is protecting me. I always thought someone would look out far more for Carl, and Dad would look out far more for me. It did seem quite normal to me.

The story of their family told by Joan and Jim

Their maternal family history

Joan: *My maternal grandmother was quite a coarse woman; she had market stalls, fruit and veg stalls. My grandfather was clearly a very bright man, although neither of them had any formal education beyond, I suppose, leaving school at fourteen? He bought a fruit farm in the early 1930s, so then they produced their own fruit which they sold in Covent Garden. He did all sorts of entrepreneurial things and made a lot of money. My mother was their only child and clearly very spoilt. My maternal grandfather had a very close bond with her and took her travelling on business trips to France. She translated for him, as her French was good. The bond between my grandmother and my mother was almost nonexistent. Gran was jealous, the wolf in the party, quite a cruel lady. Work was ingrained into her from a very early age with her three sisters. One never married and lived with Gran when she was widowed. They loathed each other. Gran actually paid her because she was frightened to live on her own.*

Gran wasn't at all loving as a mother. She did not like her daughter's husband, my father, because she didn't think he was good enough for her even though he was above her in society! Grandmother spoke her mind, particularly to her daughter's husband! When my Grandma died my mother admitted that she could not shed a tear. So, for a year or so of his life, my Dad did not have to contend with this constant bad behaviour and rejection from Gran he had endured for thirty-eight years of their married life before he died too.

Jim: *Mother was quite a peculiar person. She was the only daughter of a gypsy. Her father was born in a caravan and had raised himself from being nothing. He wasn't illiterate. He had no education. He raised himself to become a successful businessman and a landowner. He had barrows in Covent Garden, wholesale shops, and bought a farm to supply the shops. That was where we were born.*

   Mum moved from that origin to going to university as a woman in the twenties, which was extremely rare. So she made a huge social leap. My grandfather focused his whole reason for living on to his daughter, my mother. I suspect that the relationship between them was incestuous. My mother had a big secret, which she never revealed, and she committed suicide at the age of eighty-five, about two years ago. Two or three days before that I felt she was trying to say it but I was too stupid to pick it up, and then three days later she had killed herself. So there is a secret that we will never understand. My Mum's psyche was rooted in land; a very primitive pre-Christian attachment to land. She didn't have the idea of other people. There is a phrase in Africa, which is Zulu, and says that a person is a person because of people. My Mum didn't understand that at all. As far as she was concerned it was blood, family blood and land. I loved the soil. So, having left home and the farm, I didn't have anywhere to be, so I identify strongly with refugees from Kosovo. Gypsies; they don't have a place to be. That's all to do with my mother. She was the strongest influence. We were small landowners in this community, so we had status, as my parents employed other people.

Their paternal family history

Joan: *My father had an incredibly difficult childhood with not even enough food in the house. My paternal grandfather was a metallurgy teacher. He was very much a gentleman and courteous to the extreme. I would have imagined he had a kind of apprenticeship, not an education as such. He had great skills, a master craftsman with metal, and made beautiful things out of silver. I think he was quite difficult. He was a complete contrast to his wife, my paternal Grandma, who was a coarse, fish-wifey sort of person. Certainly she hadn't any education, was very hardworking, probably a housemaid. She died relatively young, no doubt from the burden of having had eight children in twelve years, four boys and four girls. My father was about third or fourth. The one he was closest to was his youngest sister, Kitty, who, curiously, is the one I am closest to. She came to help me when my first child was born because my mother wasn't free, as she couldn't leave the farm. Kitty was devastated when Dad died. I suppose that was a much stronger bond, a daughter–father bond rather than a brother–sister bond or an aunty–niece bond. I have a strong attachment to Kitty. I am still very attached to her. Her sisters were very jealous of her relationship with my father (their brother). She was the baby and he was the oldest of the boys. When Kitty was born, he would have been five or six. He looked after her and there was a bond from the beginning.*

My paternal grandfather was regularly cavorting with other women while our Granny was being totally worn out. So my grandmother used to take the baby and leave her on the doorstep of the house that she knew the house he was in, as a reminder that there were babies at home and he should come back and look after his first wife and family. They weren't well off because I imagine if he was making any money he spent it on other women and drinking.

Their parents' marriage

Joan: *My Dad went on to make an extremely close marriage of his own to Mum, much to the amazement of his brothers and sisters. They were raucous and having a jolly twenties time and some of the sisters had just done typing courses, whereas Mum was cultured, clever, and quietly spoken. They were very nice to her, and when my father died my Mum then admitted that, although she felt critical of them, she realized that they almost treated her like another sister. They would have been much more attentive had she allowed them, but she kept them at a distance. She had some very close women friends in college, but my father didn't like some of them so he wouldn't let them come and visit, which I think is dreadful. He viewed them as a threat, I realize, to their relationship, as, without exception, her friends were all single women, with good brains and education doing clever demanding jobs like teaching and nursing.*

Our father was a wonderful performer and showman and when he wasn't busy working he was actually entertaining people. He got very involved with Scouts and Rotary and he stood as a Liberal candidate. I'm sure what attracted to him to teaching was his desire to entertain. He went to university and did a maths degree, where he met my mother. He then went into the navy for a short spell, but in fact he didn't like being told what to do. He had a terrible temper. My Mum never raised her voice, ever. She had a deft use of words. She could say the most horrible things very quietly. Dad was frightening. He would lose his temper and shout at the animals [laughs]. Jim is a real gentleman and gentle, not at all with Dad's fiery temper.

My mother was very tough, but was very conscious of her role as a teacher, and a role model she maybe carried through almost to excess. She would correct our speech and our manners. My father died in 1973. So then my mother was very miserable and had twenty-five years or so before she died, and she killed herself. She took an overdose. I don't know why. She died in 1997. She didn't write a note or anything, but she wrote on the bottom of the shopping list, "I've had a sort of nightmare". It was suicide. I feel certain that, throughout her widowhood, my mother remained totally in love and committed to my father.

Jim: *What happened was that when my mother went to college she met my father. Grandfather treated this relationship immediately as hostile and he wouldn't recognize the relationship. It was an absolute taboo. He said that he felt their family was a limited company of three, that is the Dad, the mother and my Mum. Indeed, my grandfather said he would shoot my father. My father believed that. So my Mum and Dad kept their relationship secret for years, got married secretly and denied their relationship. My Mum was a teacher using her maiden name, lying about the fact that she was married. So secrets and lies in families is a very strong theme with me. This gypsy background was a closed society against a world perceived as hostile.*

After eleven years of being with my Dad, my mother's father died and they had children, me and Joan. It was a great shock to have twins. When Grandfather died my mother also managed to persuade my father, who really knew nothing about farming at all, that he would enjoy being a farmer more than he would enjoy being a teacher, and he, my Dad, my Mum and Grandma having awful conflicts, an absolute cauldron, and then into that, to make matters worse, two babies arrived.

Mother didn't give us recognition because her father had given her the idea that she wasn't allowed to relate to anyone outside the tribe or have children: so she was in this appalling dilemma with these two demanding children. My sister was ill and had to go off to a nursing home when we were little. The voice of my Mum's father inside her was telling her that other people outside of her paternal family of three don't exist, so I got a message from my Mum that I didn't exist. I found that very difficult to cope with. I am angry and that pattern has been replicated in my subsequent life. I am very angry to the degree of being able to commit murder.

My mother's reaction all through our growing up time was to contain this conflict within herself. The manifestation was that she had itching and scratching all over herself as a result of trying to respond to this unresolvable conflict with a stiff upper lip. She went to Harley Street. It was at a huge financial cost.

Their younger brother

Joan: *Jim feels that he had a very troubled relationship with my parents, and particularly with my mother. I knew nothing about it until my mother told me—that it transpires that for years he has been having private psychiatric help in London. Jim will say she saw in our brother, Jack, a reflection of her own father, an entrepreneurial businessman with quite a lot of flair for making money out of all sorts of unusual things, and that's what she sort of nurtured in Jack; to the extent that she would do things for him that she didn't do for us. Jack went on relying on our Mum to bail him out even when he was an adult.*

Jim: *Basically, what Mum did was to reproduce her father. She attributed to her son, Jack, all the characteristics of her father. She effectively turned him into a sort of modern day gypsy spiv. I felt very jealous. I was always compared adversely with him just as my father had been compared adversely with Grandfather. He is an interesting character really, he is a very well educated yobbo. He was like her father. She went all silly, like a fourteen-year-old star-struck schoolgirl. Joan is also very angry.*

School and work

Joan: *My Mum and I actually went to the same school. I did exactly what my Mum did all those years before. We were both head girl. It certainly wasn't based on academic prowess. I left school with two A levels. I spent a lot of time in music. I was arranging assemblies each morning, making sure the right people were there; but at the expense of my schoolwork. I struggled with university in agriculture. I always felt I was being unfavourably compared with Jim, who was certainly brighter. But oddly, in the end, at degree level I got a second, and he got a third [laughs]. Jack went to Cambridge, eligibly cleverer than both of us, but he only got a third because he just messed around and had a nice time.*

   My choice of work wasn't a conscious change of career. I had actually child-minded a baby who was severely handicapped. That child is now twenty-two and lives in a supported housing situation. I felt a much greater affinity with children who needed help because, I suppose, of bringing up children of my own. I found that I had much more patience working with handicapped children, for whom every simple task resembles the ascent of Everest, whereas with my own children, able, bright children, I expected them to be able to do things, so I am sure that I wasn't as patient when they were children growing up.

Jim: *I did a degree in English; I then went to Africa doing agricultural development. After that I did three years studying agriculture. I've never been able to work in a conventional work environment. I call myself an agricultural manager. So a lot of my work is actually about differentiation and negotiating relationships [laughs]. I'm very happy that I have access to lots of different work opportunities in different parts of the country. I've had a sort of public school education. My experience was being the son of a landowner so having status there. When I went to Africa after college as a VSO volunteer I suddenly realized what all this public school mumbo jumbo education was about. It was about running the Empire and I found that I could do it. I was actually rather good at it. Unfortunately, while I was there they got independence [laughs].*

   The farm wasn't making enough money to employ me. I could see that it had made my parents very unhappy; I had to do something else. Because my twin was a girl, she hadn't had all this conditioning about being the son and heir. She married someone who is an agriculturist. I went to work in London and then approached the ILEA to give me some money to study agriculture. So I was sort of zigging and zagging in and out of farming. Being a farmer's son and being the son and heir and yet having to differentiate and do something different. This pattern is parallel with the twin thing.

Their marriages and family life

Joan: *I've got five children. I have been a full time mother. I hadn't worked until my youngest child was seven. I'm willing to try out anything with a child no matter how handicapped they may be. I don't think I make a connection between this and being a twin. I also help a friend who was at college with me, and is now running a bed and breakfast. I've relied totally on my husband financially and I've developed a lifestyle to fit in with what he chose to do. It involves tons and tons of travelling in dozens and dozens of countries, and I've been the one to stay at home with the children, who take much more notice of my authority. I am very fit physically. I don't really miss my husband but I do have an amazingly strong group of women friends.*

Jim *I'm married and I've got two boys. It's my second marriage; my wife is Joan, coincidentally, because my sister is called Joan. I have sleepless nights all the time and worrying about how I am going to deliver this work. I had this feeling of disintegration. I feel I need my twin there all the time so I've sort of an identity. The social kind of pressure, especially on men in society, is to be orientated towards a goal and I have no frame of reference because I am thinking about "us" all the time. The problem is that we can't sleep, and that is a terrible burden. And we haven't solved it so we're really tired. If I sleep well my wife has a sleepless night and if she sleeps well I have a sleepless night. Just like a see-saw. We have created a situation at home where it is physically impossible to have people visit because the house is so small. So we can't have pets, and our sons can't have friends to the house. They can't have a lot of things that they want because there isn't anywhere to put them. One son wants a drum kit and a shed to put his stuff in and he wants a bit of land. He would like to have a wood to walk about in. He gets on quite well with his brother, partly because they were a bit cut off from friends.*

Their childhood and being an opposite sex twin

Joan: *At birth-time as twins we were so close, but we weren't particularly close as children growing up. Sort of normal brother–sister relationship and we were certainly closer to each other than either of us were to Jack, Jim and I. Now we're on very good terms with each other since his second marriage to Joan. As babies we were dressed very similarly; my mother cut up things and made us identical coats, rabbit fur capes. We went around very much as a pair. I think I have a sense of closeness with my twin but I think the trouble is that my first eighteen months or two years, because I was so ill, I actually was probably a useless play companion because I was sickly. I nearly died. My parents watched one twin get bigger and fatter and thrive and they watched me stand still and get weaker and feeble and they didn't do anything about it until I was nearly dead [laughs]. I think they were just so totally overwhelmed by having two children. My mother had terrible rheumatism and was going around on all fours for about the first eight weeks after the trauma of the birth. There was very little money.*

I didn't have any fat digesting enzymes, so as fast as I was given milk it was just going through me or I was being sick so I didn't gain any weight at all. At three months old I was my birth weight and that was the stage when the GP said "She's going to die." So I was put in a baby nursing home run by two Great Ormond Street nurses who fed me every hour for four or five months and eventually the fat digesting enzyme just came and I began to digest fat and that was the turning point. I would imagine that my parents did not visit often, they probably had to do it by public transport or they may have borrowed my grandmother's car. They had very little money and they also had Jim to look after.

I can remember going to school with bits of toast in my hand because I hadn't eaten any breakfast, was over that by the time I was seven or eight. In the christening pictures when we were about eleven months old we look about the same size, which is odd.

After the illness I had caught up with my twin, Jim. My other brother is four years younger and my mother had a miscarriage in between us and him.

Jim: To say that Joan was fond of me is a misunderstanding of the way I am and the way we relate. She is just there and she is part of me so that if she disappears, I've lost part of me. I am seriously impaired by the threat of this loss. I've also had quite a lot of different sorts of therapy. I'm making a very deliberate choice to go in the direction of a single identity. It struck me it might be a bit like the decision to abstain that alcoholics and drug abusers have to make. I've had the experience of walking around London and seeing tramps lying in the gutter and thinking that's exactly how I feel. So this business of denying being a twin is a purely practical strategy for survival. You cannot go through life involving another person as part of yourself as an adult. So I'm highly motivated to advance knowledge. I was in counselling for two and a half years and it really didn't work. It's very difficult for that conceptual framework to accommodate some of these twin issues. I know there are lots of twins encountering the same sort of difficulties and I have thought there must be someone who is just a mile away.

The story of their family told by Diana and Dan

Their family story

Diana: Dan and I are thirty-eight and then there is my mum, who is about seventy-one. And I'm very close to Mum. Our two sisters have children. I've had very little to do with my family at various times in my life. Dad changed career mid life and became a businessman. I am in organizational management. Dan changed careers and is in media management.

   In the family there was no such thing as "depression". My mother was depressed. My father was a serial philanderer and she was incapable of leaving. We got the worst of it because she was rock bottom when we were young. She was incapable of physically taking care of us; consequently, life was bizarre. Outsiders saw a big home in the garden. Inside the house, no meals, nothing in the *fridge, no school uniform. If I needed to feel trust I was so anxious and stressed out before asking for help as I must not make a big thing about it.*

Dan: *Let's go back to a very quick chronology. Diana and I born in the early 1960s. When we were ten we moved to another city. My mother would say she hated every second of it because my father had an affair in the city. She had no friends, we had this large house and grounds and she spent her entire time escaping to do the horses with Diana. I think her marriage was on the rocks. My middle sister would say she had no friends, all her really close friends were in her formative years. She became a wild card, finally ending up at a Polytechnic.*

    We moved in 1973, the start of the oil crisis. We had this huge house with a central heating system. You needed a mortgage just to switch it on. Money was always tight. Dad was never there. I think he hated that house. He loved it, the status of it, and he hated the commitment of it. So none of us left the city with any regret.

Their mother

Diana: *We are having such a good relationship but I resent her enormously for being so pathetic when we were young. I can't talk to her. I've tried, it was very painful and I couldn't stop crying. Mum thinks about Dan every day. She completely babies Dan in many ways. Absolutely 100 per cent the twin girl gets the sisters and a twin brother gets the mummy.*

Their father

Dan: *I suppose the omission of Dad is as great as the admission! Mum is always talking about him. He did cause a lot of misery and grief. Dad put up with a lot of shit from us all. What bothers me is the overarching role of Dad. I don't know what's normal. My relationship with him is, I am pretty certain, at the core of many of my problems. I never quite made my peace with his death. And I know that Diana feels the same way. I feel regretful. I have a strong feeling of being cheated that we didn't have longer, but that is partly my fault! He loved us. No, that is not an issue. It is much more to do with how it manifested itself in the early years. He would never be on time for parents' day at school, he would turn up for the last ten minutes. The irony is that later on he wanted to know what I was doing. I mean, my relationship with my father, as soon as I could play his games, was tremendous. He would be coming in at two in the morning. You all right? Let's have a coffee. What? It's two o'clock in the morning! He loved arguing, and funnily enough, when I saw him with his grandchildren—different man to our growing up. I can't remember sitting on his knee or playing.*

Dad was a mean bugger, he wasn't going to pay for me to have a flat when he was going hand over fist with my twin. From my perspective, it was a constant wall of money being shunted in her direction. You know, my late father never went all the way. And funnily enough I do exactly the same thing now! I said to Diana, "I'll increase the amount I give you to £400 a month." When it came to it I make it £350!

Clearly when I was younger I'd speak to Dad most days. If you got a B why wasn't it an A? A lot of that! Dad would say we're getting rid of the office typewriter and I would say oh I would like that. I taught myself to type. He said, "Can you type?" "Yes of course I can type!" "Can you type this letter for me?" Thank God for self-correcting ribbons. I'd bash these letters out for him on an old manual. When the office junior was away I would have a week of answering the phones for £50. One thing led to another. I made my peace with him on his deathbed. It was an awful time, he said you are my son, you never have to ask for forgiveness.

School and work

Diana *Dan actually failed to get into the grammar school, but he got lots of private schooling, and he overcame his dyslexia, and then went on to be very successful. There was a lot of pressure on Dan to do well. I was just completely neglected and left to do my own thing. I was just abandoned but when I had done my degree and was getting divorced, Dad realized that this girl was going to have to work for the rest of her life. She did brilliantly academically. It is such a shame, she could have gone to Cambridge. The one good thing is I always had a sparkling career.*

Dan: *It was a shock when I failed my O level exams. It's because I had been doing my hobby every hour God sends and being out with my friends. I went off to an FE college. For the first time I felt this was great. I did my O levels in a year, my A levels in a year. So I'd lost a year. I was involved with student politics and it was just great fun. Nobody took any interest. Did I work hard to justify my place at university? Absolutely, and I continued to be involved with student politics in my third year. But I had to live at home.*

Sexuality

Diana: *I told Dad about Dan's homosexuality. Dad was very angry as he thought I was telling vicious lies about my brother. Not long after, as our relationship began to develop, he began to develop his relationship with Dan and we had about eight years. I spent a lot of time with Dad on our own, and Dad spent time with Dan. Mum was there and couldn't believe that Dad, the homophobic man who loves women, was helping my brother.*

Health and addiction

Diana: *Two years ago Dan completely changed his life since he left rehab. I didn't go to rehab for my addictions with small children to look after. I've also had an eating disorder for which I have had counselling. Two months ago, the GP agreed to antidepressants. It completely changed my life.*

Dan: *What flowed from treatment was that Diana and I had a few very traumatic discussions in which it became clear to me and her that we had both seen our childhood in very different ways. Our perceptions had been quite opposite. She was just finishing her divorce with her first husband and had been through another disastrous relationship.*

   The family has the view of Diana as a rebel rouser and I don't think she would disagree with that. For some reason best known to my late father, they gave in to her. My perception is that she always got and I never did. All I am doing is earning money in part time work and my hobbies. I grant that there were marital problems at the time. I had an ostrich in the sand mentality to a lot of the family. So I don't know what trauma she might have had. We had arguments, terrible, shocking, fights almost.

Diana, I would say, was more a maintenance addiction as opposed to my addiction, which was purely hedonistic. So it's just an extraordinary thing that we both went through this at the same time. I decided we were going to have this out here and now. I went round and we must have been talking till about 4 o'clock in the morning and she was crying and I was crying. She had hated the horses but had been forced to do it. My perception was that I was left on my own. Her perception of me was that I was popular and happy, while I remember switching the lights on outside for when they came back; Dad would be out.

Diana: *Dan told me he hated me because I took all my mother's attention away from him. And I said to him, I didn't want it, I felt awful and he couldn't believe it. I used to spend a lot of time with Mother. I was just like a puppet. Dan was on his own, and I felt terrible about it. We grew up with weekends like that. I wanted her to spend time with him and us together. We never had had anything to do with each other because we were pulled apart by the parents, especially by my mother. My son puts his arms round my daughter and vice versa. Me and Dan [laughs] would never even dream of it.*

Marriage and children

Diana: *My counsellor says I have a split in my personality. At work I have a sharp intellect, and I'm reliable, but in my personal relationships I allow myself to be walked all over. I was weak and vulnerable in the face of vulnerable men. I hadn't known the strategies to cope with them. But I now know professionally and personally.*

My son and daughter are nineteen months apart. I'm sure I raised mine as virtually the same as twins. Child-care is so much easier because what you are doing for one you might as well be doing for two, so I think it was very much practical. They're best friends, with lots of hugging, support, and fun in spite of their parents' divorce. They get on with their Dad too.

Dan: *I used to see Diana with her boyfriends or her husbands. She would fly off the handle. You would never be sure with Diana. She would just lose it. But she is very bright. Much brighter than me but no tolerance whatever. She would have made a wonderful politician. She is completely blinkered to her own view. Whereas with my profession, I am constantly questioning other people even though I have my private view.*

Friendships

Diana: *I have important girlfriends, many lifelong girlfriends. They have felt that they're the waifs and strays. I have the same story of family neglect. My latest friend has the same story, but is my intellectual equal, if not my superior.*

Dan: *For much of my life the family have been out of sight out of mind. They are central, they are not core. It can't have been as grim as all that. At sixteen things changed and I had a girlfriend. By that stage I had pretty much severed my links with my old friends from before ten. I would say that 10–12 were grim. Dead, they were. I had some friends, but if I wasn't going on my bicycle over to them they didn't come over. The reality is that I am having a better social life than ever. I've been everywhere and nowhere.*

Diana: *I used to spend a lot of time with Mother. I was just like a puppet. Dan was on his own, and I felt terrible about it. We grew up with weekends like that.*

Being opposite sex twins

Diana: *I am the eldest twin by seven minutes and I gather it is because of the position we were lying in. It was a difficult birth. I was a much smaller baby than Dan although we were both big babies. There were concerns about Dan. I was very athletic and sporty like my Dad, won all the medals on the sports day and Dan was very badly co-ordinated. He was bullied in school. He still has a lot of problems with his handwriting and so do I. We are both dyslexic. We disguised our spelling with sloppy writing like my father.*

Dan is a very swift personality. He is not close to me but he's closer to me than the rest of the family, but I'm not sure whether I feel closer to him than the rest of the family. The one I feel most close to is my mother, and yet I have put her at a distance. I don't feel so close to Dan, but he is just such an integral part of my life. In the last few years we have taken to having joint birthday parties. The only thing I can say is that out of the drugs has come the light.

Dan: *Diana would go to night clubs and I was sort of the boring old fart working. I was not hip. I had never been cool in my life. Until probably now. I used to sort of admire my late grandfather, who was a very austere, correct man, polished shoes and bowler hat. I'm not like that now.*

The history of our relationship is lots of aggression. But overarching we are together whether we like it or not. Everybody always wanted to know which one of us was born first. Conflict and love are together. We are a unit, and our lives will always be intertwined and encircling and that is why the rest of the family is on the outside. We will be together, bonded in some way, because we were twins. I don't get on better with her than with my other sisters. But at the same time Diana is my twin. I never know whether we are going to be friendly when we speak. That separates us but also joins us. I would say we had no relationship at all from 16–35. She didn't quite call me sissy boy but she clearly wasn't very impressed with me as a brother. She perceived me as being the one that was favoured by Mum and Dad. Very odd that. And I said, how can you say that, they were never there. Oh, but they always talked about you. No, I think a lot of Diana's memories are of later, when Mum and Dad did start to take much more of an interest when I was at university. Suddenly I was somebody.

Our parents wanted a son and they ended up with twins. Another daughter . . . you know. I cannot recall that ever being a factor because I can't remember being favoured. It would be nice to be sitting here saying well I was favoured, I got everything I needed. There are two girls. You have another child. They wanted a boy.

My reflections on all these stories

These moving family stories, in many respects, are not different to other families, but they were experienced through the eyes of opposite sex twins. The purpose of this research is the relationship experiences of opposite sex twins and that is why these stories need to be here. In this chapter, we can see that the life of the family group preceded the life of the twins. Culture, education, parental influence, sibling relationship, and attachment produced an appropriate family member in each of the opposite sex twins, who were groomed to fulfil the roles of their gender and place in the family. These roles of these twins, as for all members of the family, were socially important for the upward mobility of the family, and biologically important for the continuation of the species.

However, there was a chasm between public and private roles within these opposite sex twins. In Chapter One and in this chapter, it is shown how opposite sex twins may have been difficult to manage for parents because of their own oedipal and marital difficulties. However, in these stories, the impact of the parental experience affected these opposite sex twins. The parental relationship experiences were particularly difficult to manage, although not unlike so many other marriages. Here, the parents were unhappy; the fathers out or angry, the mothers depressed. Splitting was a way by which marriages could survive their differences. But splitting in opposite sex twins was deeply serious; it was a failure of development maturation. It sustained far deeper, muddy furrows in the psyche, with the despairing unrequited resolution of opposite sex twin/self, who may have adopted a false self. So, the survival of the pack took precedence, but the hidden was pernicious. Questions arose. Was the participation of this particular group of opposite sex twins related to the capacity of their parents to stay together through all their stress, struggle, and pain? Did the survival of the parental relationships influence the opposite sex twin pairs in having the courage to take part in this research, which led them to sharing intimate and sometimes painful experiences of being an opposite sex twin? Was there a hope of finding some reparation for their twinship and themselves, as their parents had each done? This can only be wondered at.

Chapter Eight explores how the opposite sex twins saw themselves as similar and different to other siblings and twins. This comparison does not include children bereaved of a twin (Hayton, 2007; Woodward, 1998), or the experience of physical or mental disability of children in the family. Nor has it included the experience of only children whose experience of the absence of siblings was beyond the family experience of this group of opposite sex twins.

CHAPTER EIGHT

The opposite sex twins' similarity to, and difference from, siblings and same sex twins

> VIOLA: I am all the daughters of my father's house
> And all the brothers too; and yet I know not.
>
> (Shakespeare, *Twelfth Night*, 1601, 2.5: 122–123)

T hroughout the research, these opposite sex twins gave much thought to their impact on the family, their parents and siblings, as well as to their similarities and differences to their siblings and to other twins.

Their similarities to other siblings and twins

1. Birth order was significant for all siblings and twins.
2. Sharing was influenced by age, gender, and cultural expectation.
3. Fighting was engaged in by all children, including twins, who could demonize older siblings and fought younger siblings.
4. Fitting in was sought by everyone through the need to find commonality, and to clarify the phenomena of being themselves.

5.   It felt almost impossible to answer with words what it was like to be themselves *as this is just the way we are* (Carl). They knew no different.
6.   Their perception of each other's profession was accurate.
7.   They communicated their professional role effectively through how they behaved and what they did.

Their similarities to same sex twins

1.   The principle architecture of being a twin pair was the same and different.
2.   Shared space for all twins was not primarily separate, but shared from conception in the womb chamber.
3.   The main family focus was experienced to be on the other twin; so was the focus of the watching twin.
4.   Relating to others individually without having to share with their twin was diminished for all twins by the presence of their twin, but it was also magnified by a larger social network.
5.   Twins had the same age and same sex friends.

Joan: *There is more emphasis on letting the twins be together these days.* [This was disputed.]
Dan: *There is a greater emphasis with twins to ensure that they develop as individuals, not as a collective!*
Jim: *There is no middle ground.*

This last comment meant that they related wide apart or very close. This could be difficult. The impact of being an opposite sex twin on the family was similar to same sex twins in time, food consumption, and double the amount of care.

The differences of opposite sex twins to same sex twins

Opposite sex twins also had access to their twin's friends of the opposite sex.

Diana: *The relationships of opposite sex twins differs from the rest of the population that has had an opposite sex sibling because when they are very young small age differences make a big difference. A class above or below, they won't play with each other. You don't make friends with your siblings' friends because you are not equals. Whereas we made friends with our twin's friends because they were equals, they were the same age (and the opposite sex)!*

Same sex monozygotic twins tended to be seen as alike, but opposite sex twins tend to be seen as different. They often wondered if their experience was like that of the general public. The taboo of incest was not seen to be present for same sex twins.

The effects of opposite sex twins on the family as opposed to same sex twins

The impact of being an opposite sex twin on the family is different to same sex twins.

Joan: *We are similar to same sex twins [but] an added expense.*

Dan: *I think it is much easier for two same sex twins to become as one. They can share clothes, we couldn't, or activities, friends, and entertainment.*

Diana: *With opposite sex twins there's a different effect on the family, particularly on the parents who are the opposite sex. If you have got two children and they are male and female, then if the mother would really rather play with the female, then she has got the female, or the other way round.*

They often wondered if their experience was like the general public.

Jim: *Is it just one of the facts of modern life, that people feel to some degree alienated and marginal, or is it specifically to do with being an opposite sex twin?*

CHAPTER NINE

The archive of the findings

OLIVIA: Most Wonderful!

(Shakespeare, *Twelfth Night*, 1601, 5.1: 234)

T his chapter discusses the surprising relationship experiences that emerged from the previous chapters. These experiences do not necessarily belong to all the opposite sex twins of this research. However, where they were not disputed, they have been included. Where there was dispute, the disputes are discussed. These relational themes illuminate the literature in Chapter One, which, in turn, validates and challenges them leaving a sense of tantalizing fascination. Themes are herewith summarized in Figure 11 and the following subtitles: the infant years; the social world; and, the cultural versus the embodied influences.

The infant years

1. The architecture of opposite sex twinship.
2. Individuation.
3. Attachment for opposite sex twins.
4. A panoramic view.

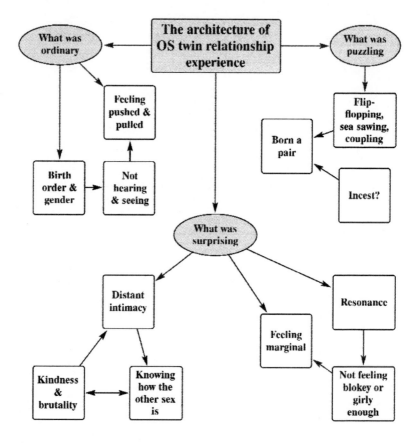

Figure 11. The findings from the research.

The social world

1. The status of gender.
2. Being equals.
3. Pulled apart or pushed together.
4. The parental influence.
5. Siblings.
6. The fighting of opposite sex twins.
7. Coupling or flip-flopping.
8. Relationships.

The cultural vs. the embodied influences

1. The taboo of incest and intimacy.
2. Marginality.
3. The taboo of resonance.
4. Brutality.

The infant years

The architecture of twinship is different from that of singletons. Furthermore, twinship has its own peculiar architecture when the twins are opposite sex. This is exemplified in the requirements of biology and culture for the human species to grow up to find their other half for procreation. Jim said, *what do you do if you've already got one of those?* These opposite sex twins are expected to find a partner of the same sex as their opposite sex twin, but in childhood they have not tended to be expected to play with each other. This makes for a contradictory confusion about the other gender in the complex journey of growing up. The solution these opposite sex twins adopt is to believe they have to learn *individuation*.

Individuation

The architecture of twinship sits uneasily with the principle of individuation. Individuation requires an infant to experience a separate and distinct existence before the baby experiences attachment with mother (Chapter One). Individuation is understood as a necessary psychic step to intimacy between two persons to avoid symbiosis or a fusion of two selves. For opposite sex twins, individuation creates what Jim called a *Darwinian crisis . . . they are born as a pair but the world is not cut out for pairs, especially not opposite sex twin pairs.* They have to learn to be single. To do this, opposite sex twins try to adopt a false self by cutting off the essence of their opposite sex twinship. They believe they cannot learn an individuated self that includes the unique essences of opposite sex twinship. There is a curious consequential outcome of this in the research. The capacity of these opposite sex twins to relate to the emotional state of people they are not close to, or "twinned" with, does not appear accurate. It is not surprising. They cannot be accurate about themselves, so how can they be accurate about others? This is a cruel falsehood. The group expressed shame at failing to individuate like singletons.

Attachment for opposite sex twins

The architecture of infant attachment is different for opposite sex twins. Before birth, all twins are already in deep "attunement". As Freud observed: "The ego is first and foremost a bodily ego derived from bodily sensations, chiefly springing from the surface of the body . . . developing a sense of self" (Freud, 1923, p. 26). Twin image, as part of the sense of twin self, is deeply embedded in body tissue before the twins are born. It is a seeing and hearing beyond eyes and ears. There are: "Inter-changes in utero, based on sensing, not perceiving before and after birth . . . The twins are always present for each other" (Piontelli, 2002, pp. 50–51). Once the twins are born, mother tries to look at them, gazing on one infant twin while holding the other twin in mind, but she can never be entirely present and possessed, in love or in reverie, to and by one infant. Ideally, she needs to be in love or reverie with both twins at the same time. This means a different intimacy of distance, because for the opposite sex twins to be a singleton with mother is to kill off the other twin in their minds. At a fantasy level, it may be desirous but it is also disastrous as so many lone twins bear witness to (Hayton, 2007). Diana explained: *Dan told me he hated me because I took all my mother's attention away from him. And I said to him, I didn't want it, I felt awful and he couldn't believe it.* If possession is part of the primary attachment between baby and mother, then possession for twins is triangular after birth, and dyadic, or a relationship of two, before birth. It can be argued that, even before birth, the relationship is triangular, as mother holds the infants in her womb and in her mind. The twins relate to each other within the womb–mother. Ultrasound indicates that twins may sense this womb in which they are held. It is primitive and intense, as the twin experience is part of the self. Once born, a twin has to survive both the loss of the twin/self, and being deprived of the steady mother/womb/feeder. The feeling of separation and hatred for their twin half is not like losing or hating a mother or father. It is more primitive and intense.

This does not mean that the loss of mother/womb is not also powerful.

Equality does not reign for any twins in the womb. One twin may receive more sustenance than the other.

> Even assuming that maternal "stressors", of whatever origin and kind, can reach the foetus, twin foetuses would only receive the same quality, but never the same quantity, of such substances . . . Twin foetuses have different umbilical cords as well as an unequal distribution of placental mass . . . and differing blood flows. [Piontelli, 2002, p. 49]

Differences start early, indeed, as do the remarkable similarities between opposite sex twins that are illuminated in this research and, surprisingly, appear to complement the biological, behavioural, and psychotherapy literature discussed in Chapter One.

A panoramic view

To return to Workshops 1 and 2, described as a playpen or a mother womb, the group seemed "fed" by their experience from the Workshops. The Workshops provided a secure base from which to explore and reflect on their relationships. Sandbank observed that the basis of infant–mother attachment through reverie (Bowlby, 1988) may be less secure for twins in comparison to the single baby's experience of having mother to themselves. Lacombe (1959) saw this lack of infant–mother relationship for twins as a deficit of attunement and, therefore, of regulation in infant twins. However, as McDonald (2001) observed, threes are twos for twins; twin–twin and mother, twin–twin/mother, or mother/twin–twin. This is the hub of twin relationship attachment. It is then further complicated by gender expectations for opposite sex twins that are driven by socio-genetic forces.

However, these opposite sex twins did not appear to compensate for the possession deficit of being a single baby with mother. They did something else. Their view was panoramic. They did this by encompassing body–eye gazing of the twin–mother together in their mind. In the workshops, the opposite sex twins kept their eye on their twin and spoke to the researcher at the same time, or the other way around. For these opposite sex twins, attachment was in threes. It was a panoramic relationship view of the world. They were coupled in a three.

As part of this panoramic view, the opposite sex twins could be like "teddy bears" to their twins, and, later, to others. As such "the twin could be a transitional object" (Sandbank, 1999. p. 168) that knew the most private, even unconscious, moments of each other. The teddy bear role captured the way in which these opposite sex twins provided part of their secure base for their twin and self. They knew how to resonate with a person close to them, even to embody another's feelings if they were paired with them, especially if of the opposite sex. This they did superbly well. Dan said, *It is like the film* What Every Woman Wants, *where a male finds he can hear the thoughts of women.* The opposite sex twins' capacity to tune into each other was part of their play. This could happen between any two people, but was surprising here between these opposite sex twins, who described themselves as primarily feeling distant to each other.

Dan: *She has taken refuge in the chocolate!*
Diana: *At this point!* [laughs].
Dan: *Nothing else left!*
Diana: *Nothing else left, no, no!*
Dan: *Other than Cadburys Dairy Milk . . .*

They found it less easy to anticipate how others felt with whom they were not twinned. This might be because they had not been able to embrace an empathy and warmth towards their own opposite sex twinship as part of their sense of a secure base of self from which to reach out.

Their social world

The status of gender

The status of gender, and, therefore, of being an opposite sex twin, was not the same for men as for women. The men did not feel proud of being an opposite sex twin. The women felt they had status by having a twin brother. Not so their brothers. The men did not express a sense of prestige by having a twin sister; almost the reverse, they were lumbered. They thought there would be more status in having a twin brother than a twin sister. None the less, the men still wanted the support of their twin sister, who tried to reciprocate in the role of twin–mother. The women wanted to depend on their twin brother for support but also saw their weaker side. The men were unsure on whom to depend, as they were not meant to depend on their female twin. But, although the men seemed less influenced by the women, they deferred to them, followed them, and watched them.

The constrictions of status could cause hatred that was exacerbated by a denial of their opposite sex twinship. How far this was driven by a parental preference for boys, or social–trans-generational–genetic–biological influences, is hard to know. These opposite sex twins were faced with the pressure of status from social expectations without and within at an increased intensity compared to other children. It was not straightforward. The status quo of opposite sex twin male supremacy was thrown into disarray by these opposite sex twin women, who tended to develop more quickly and were often first to the task. So, status was a source of disappointment to them both. Again, the men tended to think they would feel more status with a twin brother they could really compete with. They did not feel as threatened by their twin sister, nor do they feel admired. The women also felt deprived of admiring the men, but curiously made no indication of their need to be admired. Was this influenced by their feelings of not being admired by their opposite sex twin? The women wanted to be seen as equal to their twin, but the best they could get was to be twin–mother. So, neither of them could really sharpen their claws and find their strength, nor could they enjoy their unique twinship. The plot thickened.

Being equals

As children, they were the same age, yet they could not compete with each other because they were expected to be opposite sex. Meanwhile, these opposite sex twins had more exposure to the friends of their opposite sex twin, so they had more friends of the opposite sex than other children. I anticipated the gender difference to be one of the most difficult and tricky of the opposite sex twin dilemmas. Non-matching duets summed up the requirements to be different and separate and were another reason as to why the opposite sex twins felt pushed together and pulled apart.

Pushed together or pulled apart

The parental influence

The opposite sex twin couple may have been treated as a mirror of the parental couple. This could cause confusion for each twin, as well as the opposite sex twinship, which could have had little space to resolve its own relationship. The complexity of the parental couple's response to their children, but especially to opposite sex twins, could have a strong influence on the sense of the opposite sex twins being pushed together and pulled apart. Unconscious processes of warring parents could project their distress on to and into any one or both of the twins individually and as a pair. This could happen with any twins or siblings, but would have a special effect on opposite sex twins, who appeared most to mirror the parental couple. In turn, they could also unconsciously enact the parental drama that might excite more pain and displeasure in their parents as well as in themselves. The buck did not stop there. Schutzenberger (1998), one of the pioneers of trans-generational psychotherapy, revealed the hidden links in family trees that unconsciously get passed down through generations. This fascinating work was beyond the remit of this book, but I wanted to draw attention to the notion that all relational difficulties could have a wider panoramic pattern of relational influence than those present in the moment. The importance of this is not to apportion blame, but to extend compassion to an historical sequel of relational pain that could end up residing in these opposite sex twins, as can be seen in any human story.

If parental couples were not happy together, as was seen in this research, the opposite sex twins could carry the stress. Generally, the influence of one parent at a time on one child, or the parental couple on the individual child, is what is considered. The influence of the parental pair on the dynamics of a pair of children, in this case the opposite sex twins' pair, is not generally thought about. Here, part of the individuality of opposite sex twins is that they are a pair, therefore the influence of the role of the parental pair on the opposite sex twins as a pair needs to be thought about. The parents of these opposite sex twins were not experienced as close. Times were hard, and there was parental strife when the opposite sex twins were little. The thoughts of these opposite sex twins about the influence of their parents were individually based. It was what they were brought up to. Dan saw himself like an ostrich towards the family, and saw that he used to be like one of his grandfathers. He also thought he was like his father. Jim felt full of rage, like his father and maternal grandfather, but did not see himself as like them. He appeared to hate his mother. Carl saw himself as sensitive, like his mother. Clare saw herself like her father. She definitely did not want to be like her mother, nor did Diana or Joan. None of them saw their twinship as a mirror of the relationship of their parents. Diana thought *the parents get the chance to play with a twin of either sex*. However, in response to her own upbringing, Diana, a single mother, did set out to encourage her children to be close to each other, to her and their father, her divorced husband.

Siblings

Having brought attention to the importance of the parental relationships to these opposite sex twins, their sibling experiences also affected them. They were play-objects for their siblings. *We were toys; they used to chuck us around* (Clare). Other twins were expected to play together, these opposite sex twins tended not to be. The activities they did or were expected to do together were pragmatic: *Those of circumstance, such as coming home from school and seeing each other in the playground* (Dan). If they did play, they seemed to get separated by the order of sibling favourite or the needs of the parents and other siblings. This is true for all members of a family, but had its own peculiarity when the opposite sex twinship was not given its share of time and space. So the normal push and pull could be confusing. This then was enacted by the opposite sex twins themselves. Frustration had to be managed by all family members, but the frustration for these opposite sex twins was more complex as individuals and as a pair: gender issues, equality, parental influence as individuals and a pair, being an opposite sex pair but not being a pair, lead to *push and pull*, as they described it.

In this research, the possibility of spontaneous play between opposite sex twins was also interrupted by the demands of the workshop activities pushing and pulling the opposite sex twins to attend to another research task. The opposite sex twins could not follow through on the more hidden task of discovering their opposite sex twin relationship in their own way. Things were never single, never quite how they seemed, quite often the opposite. This was embodied by the request of the opposite sex twins not to be with their twin too much, but, on the other hand, they were watching them all the time. *I was more curious as to what my twin did, as I knew what I did* (Dan).

They felt pushed together or pulled apart with *no middle ground. Middle ground* was arrived at through finding their place in relationship to their parental and their sibling position as well as their twinship. Middle ground is negotiated through play. Play seemed to be limited and frustrated for these opposite sex twins. Even the opposite sex twins in the group stopped playing, as they chortled together,

Dan: *Anyway, enough of us!*
Diana: *Enough of us!*

As researcher, I asked the group to consent to planned workshop structures. Neither I nor they suggested we would just see what happened. The fear of containing the *volcano* seemed driven by notions of not knowing how to think about two at a time, as Jim so vividly described. There was only room for ones. To move to living in a world with two twins meant living at a different pace. Let me illustrate this point. A musical soloist can get the orchestra to quicken or slow down, according to his whim. In a duet, the soloists are moderated and inspired by each other, which in turn guides the orchestra. It is not quite this straightforward. Behind this musical moment are the composer, the conductor, and the orchestra, who influence the duet. The volcanic fear appeared somewhat cut off from context. Perhaps the experience of being an opposite sex twin felt unrelated to the rest of the world as their twinship could not be thought about and, therefore, was felt as anarchic. This could stir mounting levels of anxiety that could feel volcanic. Opposite sex twins are not the same as the rest of the world. They did not come single into this world and they came as an opposite sex pair. Reflection about opposite sex twins has not been very apparent, so there could be a poor internalized experience of the place and role of opposite sex twin within. There was a loneliness in this. In this sparse landscape where there has been a shortage of understanding of the phenomena of opposite sex twins there has tended to be pushing, pulling, conflict, and fighting over and above that of the normal scrapping for position in the pecking order of siblings and families.

How did these opposite sex twins fight?

Fighting, in the architecture of opposite sex twins, was not the same as for other twins and siblings. For all twins, fighting was difficult. Siemon (1980) described the fear of conflict: "It's as though I will destroy myself if I'm angry at someone" (p. 396). Unlike siblings or same sex twins, these opposite sex twins did not fight each other physically. It was hard to know how much their fights were also a manifestation of the fights between the parents or other siblings. Diana said, *I didn't fight my twin brother—he was way too strong for me!*, while Dan retorted, *I was always lost. You used to taunt me for being such a weakling!* There were occasional big verbal fights in which they both ended in tears. The opposite sex twins tended to fight those weaker than themselves. Like their siblings, they also fought each other through other strategies that did not look like fighting but were forms of control, such as being the peace-keeper; appearing confused; warding off people; silence; taking opposite positions in thought; laughing at each other; making judgements; withholding or upstaging each other. They could fight in these subtle ways, but they did not often enter into direct competition, as they were of different gender. *It is not the same as having a twin brother with whom he would be compared* (Dan). The opposite sex twin men were seen as aggressive by the women, but the opposite sex twin women did not seem to recognize their own aggression; nor were they challenged by the men. However, the opposite sex twin women were usually first to act or speak, and in this they competed with, but simultaneously protected, their twin brother. The opposite sex twin men tried to represent their feelings, but the opposite sex twin women seemed hurt. They experienced each other as either wanting too much or too little of each other. There was no middle ground, leaving a curious friction. Competition was not straightforward because they were of a different sex and could not be alike. Neither of them could compete and win as they were opposite sex. There was not quite the same triumph as there could be over a same sex sibling. On the other hand, sometimes the opposite sex twins coupled, which could produce anxiety in their parents or carers.

Coupling, flip-flopping, and difference

In the literature, coupling is seen as a strategy to individuate or to attach as a defence (Bion & Foulkes, 1985). Sandbank (1988) understands "coupling" to range from a form of individuation to, at worst, a twinning that protects each twin from separation and from relating to others. Put another way, in the psycho–socio field, the concern is that at worst "the skin" between twins was "thin" while the skin around the twin pair was "thick" (Meltzer, 1975) and so kept other relationships out. This research saw twin coupling as a quest for the denied twin self. An old wisdom might parallel this phenomenon: when we grow up we may aspire to be different from our parents (twin denial) but, paradoxically, it is only when we have learnt how we are alike (twin possession) that we can know our difference. The importance of this was expressed through Davis and Davis (2004b), same sex twins earlier described. Everyone thought they were alike. They knew they were different. They found that out by "playing" together. The context for resolution of friction and violence can be worked out through play (Mitchell, 2003), so, as Engel, a same sex twin himself, communicated: "Aggression between twins can be dealt with by a delicate balance of the defences" (Engel, 1975, pp. 34–35). Here, Jim described coupling as a form of short-term problem solving that he experienced with his wife. This could be done by *Flip-flopping or see-sawing—you'll be happy, I'll be sad; you'll be asleep, I'll be awake*. It was a way of diffusing the friction. Flip-flopping allowed the opposite sex twins to role reverse, to hold feelings of the other role. In this way, they concurred with the literature.

The research provided a place to reflect upon the relationships of these opposite sex twins. In Workshop 1, there significant feelings about being an opposite sex twin were expressed by one of each pair of opposite sex twins. They were curiously matched by their own twin who *did not want* to express their feelings but did not want to be left out! It would be easy to interpret *flip-flopping* as a passive–aggressive position to avoid relating to others and miss the attempt at the discovery of self through the twin pairing. Opposite sex twinship had not been owned, so that both twins could feel three-dimensional. Hence, flip-flopping was seen as a preliminary early strategy to twin on the one hand and individuate on the other. This could be seen as a form of parasitism (Athanassiou, 1986). It was children's expression of role play. What they could not find, but the research provided, was a place to triangulate this experience of two feelings through reflection, so that they could be internalized as a positive experience between the twins and within each twin. So, they could both be different and similar at the same time. This "coupling" that fails to work through to a triangulation is familiar in so many sorts of relationships: siblings, parents, colleagues, to name but a few. It is a familiar polarization and often leads to divorce.

My first sculpture (Chapter Two) unconsciously expressed this uncompleted role play, where the head of the one child and two parents was three-dimensional; the other "twin", the peacock, was only in relief and at the back. It illustrated the outcome of flip-flopping, where there appeared one to the fore and one behind, instead of two whole infants. How common is this experience in sibling relationships? The research showed several examples where one twin spoke forth, was in the front, while the other did not, was in the back, *but* they did not want to be left out, and needed their position recognized and valued. They were appearing to hold a position of difference, but in their twin pair. However, it was not always as it seemed.

Similarity

These opposite sex twins discovered that they were having the same feelings as each other but one was not declaring it, although the other showed it by what they did. Their words, or lack of words, were an inverted flip-flopping that could, indeed, look parasitic. One twin appeared to piggy-back upon another, by appearing to be half absent. As Jim described, he tried to be different because he knew he felt the same. As the Davis twins knew, this could result in misunderstanding from others with whom, in turn, they may feel hostile. How they appeared was not necessarily all the truth. For example, the articulate child might not necessarily be the most secure child. These opposite sex twins, when they were quiet, might not only have been possibly "withdrawn", but protecting their noisy twin. Dan did not want to speak, as he knew his twin sister would be upset, but his very silence could lead to him feeling less important if his silence was not noticed and valued. In this way, each twin needed to become three-dimensional through membership of a healthy, valued arena of opposite sex twinship in which there were two whole children so they could normalize their paradox of going on together and separately at the same time, and so enter into other social and intimate relationships.

Relationships

During Workshop 1, these opposite sex twins wanted to direct their attention to the nature of intimacy and, therefore, their own relationship experiences to each other and to their partners. There was a possible bias away from other family relationships. This seemed inevitable, as none of the group had discussed their opposite sex twin relationship experience with other opposite sex twins or with each other before. In this, they had not played together. Their relationship patterns can be seen in the figures of the sociometry made at the start of Workshop 1 (see Image 8, The sociometric graph, Chapter Five).

The sociometric pattern of relationships was dominated by distant relationships. I draw attention especially to the apparent scarcity of intimate relationships. Only one twin (again) of each pair was close to mother, and none appeared close to father, and yet he was seen as very important in other parts of the research. It was an example of patterns that interwove with paradoxes everywhere. This is always to be found in long questionnaires. For example, the graph showed that the group did not feel close to their opposite sex twin, but preferred to be an opposite sex twin to same sex twinship or a singleton. They felt distant to many of their relationships, but this distance did not necessarily mean what it looked like. Diana explained in her choice of distance to her twinship:

It isn't how I feel about twinship, it is how I felt about our relationship.
Standing closer wouldn't necessarily mean that we are in a good relation-
ship. By standing at a distance it doesn't necessarily mean that we are a
bad relationship, but that we are distant from one another.

It was surprising how many of the relationship choices this
opposite sex twin group made were distant. Would it have been the
same for any group, was it a cultural demise, or peculiar to these
opposite sex twins? Thereby hangs another research in itself. Be
that as it may, it was the most striking feature of this sociometric
graph and led to thinking about the nature of intimacy for opposite
sex twins through their panoramic view.

Their panoramic view

The capacity of these opposite sex twins to view the world as a
panorama was developed through relating to their primary attachment of the twin–twin–mother triad through distance. Distance
became a form of intimacy capable of embracing the landscape of
the twin–self with the twin–mother. It later grew into another
recognized panoramic view that everyone has to learn through
embracing further relationships with father, siblings, and others.
Although father appeared distant, it did not mean he was not
important. Far from it. The power of absence was sometimes felt to
be greater than presence. This paralleled the strategy of distance
apparent in these opposite sex twins. Distance was *neither good nor*
bad (Diana). However, distance could express an implicit attempt by
opposite sex twins to hold things together, as fragmentation to a self
that was not individual was terrifying, while self as opposite sex
twin was not affirmed. The "defence" or "solution" of distance
could also be a secret and unconscious attempt to find compromise
between the cultural pressures and the hidden primitive early
connection. So, distance and panoramic viewing could be an
attempt to keep a space for roles that cannot be seen, named, or
cherished, like small, not easily detected moth holes in the lattice-
work of opposite sex twin relationship where reside the ghosts of
sensations, forbidden senses of twin, and, therefore, aspects of the
self that are all but lost. These holes can be a part of the psyche of
any member of the family. Longed for relationships are central to
human misery. All sorts of family relationships are discreet, hidden,

and at worst abusive. But none is so primitive, rooted as it is in the preverbal, pre-symbolic, and embodiment before sensation.

These opposite sex twins wondered what this distance might mean in terms of their intimate relationships. *What influence does being an opposite sex twin have on their intimate relationships* (Clare)? Distance meant it was difficult to find a middle ground. They could feel too close or too far from others. It adds another perspective to flip-flopping. This was intensified if they were having to pretend to be what they were not, to be single children. They may well have found it difficult to find their soul mate, as they had to deny the "soul mate" they were born with.

They tended to gravitate towards the opposite sex as friend and twin–mother with whom they felt most comfortable as a part of their primary sense of themselves. Clare and her twin, Carl, had played as little ones, but Clare saw herself as a daddy's girl and Carl as a mummy's boy. The twins somehow lost each other after those formative years, although, in adulthood, Carl sometimes comes to stay in Clare's house. Perhaps playing in the early years had a binding strength for each of them that was lost to the other opposite sex twins. Then their Mum had a breakdown and Dad was off at work. Did this have some bearing on what might have been a good enough internalized opposite sex twin relationship? While apparently the closest of the twin pairs, there were also the unresolved themes that have been raised through this research and tended to lead to their perception that forming intimate relationships to others was too close, too far, and with no middle ground. Clare felt she made *crap* relationships. It was confusing. She was not alone.

The cultural vs. the embodied influences

The taboo of incest and intimacy

Opposite sex twinship needs to be differentiated from incest in order to understand the nature of their intimacy. The architecture of the relationship experience of opposite sex twins is surrounded by the complexity and intensity of the realities and fantasies that are encapsulated in Gibran's discourse on marriage that sounds more like the experience of opposite sex twins: "Born together . . . even as the strings of a lute are alone they quiver with the same music"

(Gibran, 1992, pp. 18, 21). Opposite sex twins really are born together; it is not a metaphor for sexual bliss. Incest between opposite sex twins appears to be the most primitive fear for some and a fascination in others. It has led to a prohibition on opposite sex twins playing together, murder of them both, sometimes murder of the mother, but more often murder of the girl. This can be due to poverty and shortage of food, but not necessarily. On the other hand, in some cultures, an insistence has been made on the twins' marriage. They have even been deified. This has been well documented by Lewin (2004), Rosambeau (1987), and Sandbank (1988). Returning to the question of incest, there is some recognition that this prohibition protects the parents from their own powerful feelings of possession of one of the twins, usually the boy. On the other hand, Coles notes that "excessively strong sibling relationships and parental inattention or neglect go hand in hand" (Coles, 2003, p. 93). This can result in incest, but the neglect component, according to Sandbank (1988), is likely to be expressed in one twin (usually the girl) parenting the other. This role of care is seen with abandoned children living in the Indian sewers, and with the children who saw little of their parents in the early days of the Kibbutz (Bettelheim, 1969). Here, it would seem that the urge to relate for survival was more primitive than that of sex, especially, again, where food is in short supply.

However, the prohibition on opposite sex twins' intimacy is beginning to be thought about in the media, science, and psychology. In 2008, there was the tragic case of opposite sex twins, separated at birth, meeting, falling in love, and marrying, only to find that their marriage was illegal, not unlike Sigmund and Siglinda in Wagner's *Ring Cycle*. This has raised important issues about the nature of twins, adoption, rights to transparency, and the depth of pain caused to children. These painful feelings can create an overpowering tumult of embodied emotion that can become sexualized when they are reunited. The documentary, *Sleeping with my Sister*, (Channel 4, March 2008), about two pairs of reunited siblings has brought an empathy and discourse about the pain engendered that leads to genetic sexual attraction (GSA). Those researching this phenomenon have started to engage in public dialogue. This change of perspective may affect how opposite sex twins and other siblings in the family, in school, and in adult life, are treated. It also raises difficult ethical concerns in view of the prevalence of abuse. Sandbank expresses a view, held frequently in the literature, that opposite sex twins repress sexual desire for each other and that this is later expressed in their sexual relationships with others that is demonstrated in Bertolucci's film (2003) about opposite sex twins, *The Dreamers*. Comments by these opposite sex twins on incest appear to concur with Sandbank (1988) and Coles (2003), who echo the belief that close proximity prohibits incest.

In the research activities involving distance and pairing, the opposite sex twins found choosing other partners of the opposite sex brought awareness of the opposite sex of their twin, but, when raised in discussion, incest was then dismissed. The only feeling that the family allowed was *to be no more than a sibling*. This verbal response might be a defence for all the reasons already discussed, but this defence was somewhat challenged by a further comment by Jim: *There is something beyond gender difference.* Here, Jim seems to echo glimmers of similarity and possible hormonal transfer (Chapter Three).

To push out from the stricture of the taboo and fear of incest can be to reach a different consideration. As a result of ultrasound, we may now be able to understand the meaning of incest between opposite sex twins on a completely different level. It may be that sex in the womb has been witnessed, but there are other ways of considering the powerful feelings around this topic. If incest is an exchange of juices, then incest does take place in the womb: something deeper than sex happens in the exchange of hormones and other essences that form body cell and tissue. Sexual union as an activity in the womb is a question that is beyond the limits of this research, but it might be an expression of opposite sex twins being together in the womb. It might miss the possible understanding that the "union" of opposite sex twins may be pre-sexual. Opposite sex twin bodies may hum at the same time and in the same song and place, which has been expressed in this research. This is erotic, but it is not sexual.

The question of incest had further light thrown on it by the essences of these research findings in which the terminology adopted arose from the language of these opposite sex twins. The first essence was their feeling of being *marginal*.

Marginality

The architecture of marginality experienced by these opposite sex twins was of not feeling *blokey or girly* enough. This might have been influenced by the transfer of hormones in the womb, or by being around each other as opposite sex twins, or both. Thus, the private roles of *marginality*, that they all recognized, strained against the public roles of male and female status, adding a particular twist to their experience of being opposite sex twins. With *marginality* upsetting their status quo of gender, the solution could be to try to become even more different from their opposite sex twin, which magnified a false self of even greater difference that then could get acted out in other relationships and even lead to a source of anguish in daily relational life.

These opposite sex twins were surprised to find that they all felt *marginal*. The opposite sex twin men felt there were expectations to be fulfilled, and behaved in ways associated with males, just as the opposite sex twin women behaved as females. They had culturally appropriate socio–emotional thoughts, but Jim said, *It is not how they feel*. Feeling *marginal* could be a sign of our changing society, or simply part of being human, but it was baffling for these opposite sex twins, who, unlike other twins, were expected to thrive on their gender difference. However, they recognized that they did not *feel blokey or girly*. This marginality could be seen as a sign that opposite sex twins were a step ahead in the battle of the sexes. In our time, the roles of male and female have changed enormously. Men are allowed to be more feminine and women are moving up the professional status ladder. Denmark is seen as the happiest country, because it has developed an equality for male and female power (James, 2007). Added to the feelings of marginality of the opposite sex twins, the scientists are noting that opposite sex twin men are more feminine and opposite sex twin females are more masculine, due to transfer of hormones. So, the feelings of these opposite sex twins may be related to facts. Essentially, there was no opposite position, but, rather, a social expectation on the one hand and on the other a lattice of sensation, of felt but unexpressed experience of *marginality*, and, therefore, a sense of inadequacy in relation to the rest of society.

Through marginality, be it hormonal or social, it seemed nature had taken care of the incestuous dilemma. It might simply be familiarity. There was no mystery about the privacy of the other sex and their feelings.

Dan: *When other boys were round the back of the bike shed getting all excited when they discovered what a bra looked like . . .*
Joan: *You had seen far too many.*
Dan: *I had to battle through them to get to the bathroom. It was not a great achievement! It was very ordinary.*

They felt marginal. They both knew too much and yet not enough of the awe and fascination of not knowing the opposite sex. Feeling marginal for these opposite sex twins had implications for their intimate relationships and for incest. They did not appear to feel sexually interested in each other, but at the same time there was something there. As already described, historically and socially, the fantasized union of opposite sex twins has often been sexualized. Family members may feel displaced by opposite sex twins as individuals, as a pair, and as an opposite sex pair. So, opposite sex twins could be said to take on the role of a neutered ram described by Jim and Joan: *In agriculture when you are breeding sheep you get the teaser ram, who is vasectomized, is set to run with the ewes for two weeks before the real ram is introduced, so they'll do the business.*

Opposite sex twins could raise sexual fantasies that they themselves did not feel drawn to because they were too marginal. It was not that these opposite sex twins could not have sexual relationships; they simply knew too much, so they did not feel drawn to each other.

However, attuning to a singleton with a different boundary world could present difficulties because their role as opposite sex twin had not been internalized as a good experience. Unlike other twins and siblings, the experience of being an opposite sex twin was not led by a need to express difference, but a taboo on expressing similarity. There was a more fundamental connection, beyond desire, that resulted in opposite sex twins feeling not *blokey or girly* but *marginal* that could throw yet another light on incest. Their connection was deeper than sex. This was much more difficult to talk about.

Feelings of unequal gender status, preference for sons and the first-born, and the private roles of *marginality* could become a cocktail of guilt and shame that did little to engender a good experience of the self as opposite sex twin. So, the drama of being an opposite sex twin tended to be seen as difficult if not disastrous; do not go there, it will not be invigorating, reassuring, or rewarding. It is hardly surprising that opposite sex twins choose to sidestep this cocktail of confusing roles in their attempt to individuate. But they miss discovering the ingredients that sprang from this group of opposite sex twins, which appeared to allow some amelioration and arose in the embodiment dimensions of this research.

The taboo of resonance

The greatest surprise to the opposite sex twins was what they called *resonance*, repeatedly affirmed by how they moved as a pair, interacted with each other, painted, and made sociograms of similarity or complementarity. Resonance was the similarity "between" them. The recognition of resonance emerged in the dialogues of the opposite sex twins in Chapters Five and Six. They found they twinned with any member of the group they were paired with, as they did with their own twin. *They sort of fit together* (Carl). Resonance was something they had no control over; it was deeply unconscious. Resonance was not new in the field, although new to these opposite sex twins. They seemed a mirror image for each other. Sandbank (1988) notes that opposite sex twins have much in common with identical twins. Zazzo (1960) also notices what he calls a puzzling outcome. "Opposite sex twins are less alike than MZ twins but more alike than same sex twins" (pp. 243–352). The underlying expectation was that opposite sex twins would be more different than nonidentical same sex twins to identical twins. The degree to which *resonance* was prevalent among them surprised this opposite sex twins' group. These apparent similarities, marginality, and resonance appeared to correlate with some of the scientific findings described in Chapter One, and could lead to promising future research in the arts and sciences.

Resonance was deeper than relational exchange, and therefore belonged to questions yet to be answered about womb experience. Resonance was embodied deep in cell structure. Put another way, it is said that blood is thicker than water as an expression of family attachment. With opposite sex twins it is the same blood at the same time that plays its part in the beautiful architecture of opposite sex twin resonance. It is not something that an individual owns. Rather, it owns you. You are privileged to be part of it. It manifests itself in you and between you and your twin, whether you would have it so or not.

Is it possible that *resonance* is also made manifest and sexualized by distance? Is what is now called genetic sexual attraction, or GSA, the primitive connection of resonance that is so deep, or is it something else? This fascinating topic of resonance was recognized by these opposite sex twins through what they did and painted. It happened between them. It was irrepressible. One group member consistently disputed observations of resonance by the others, but at the same time sought and found 'resonance' with his group partner. These contradictions are prevalent in all relationship encounters, but none at such a primitive level as expressed in the relationship of opposite sex twins through the presence of *brutality*, the other side of the coin to *resonance*. Here, again, the shadow illuminates the foreground, as the existence of each twin magnifies the other twin. They are more than individual.

Brutality

Brutality was the experience of being left out or sidelined by their own twin in the group. Brutality could be held within one twin, within both of the twins, and between a twin pair at the same time. No moment belonged singly to one twin without the impact of that moment on the other twin, even though these twins prided themselves in not being influenced by their twin. The opposite sex twins already struggled with insecurity about their sense of true self, and then had to weather that the way things looked might not be how they felt, or vice versa. It was a complex and confusing world. Brutality was not physical, as Dan said: *like hanging from the chandelier. It is mental.*

Choice made by one twin that denied the place of the twin connection felt wrong and brutal to the other twin. They did not like where their twin put them in the group sculpts. They all complained, or dismissed their twin's choice. But they also had to put up with that because mother–researcher (myself) did not have enough time for their complaints. Time was running out, therefore so did "food". The experience of brutality was a psychic hunger. "Mother" researcher may have facilitated a very different twin experience if the opposite sex twins had been asked to make the sculpts as twins, not as individuals. They would not have been set up against each other to be different. I could have paid my dues to their primary sense of self through opposite sex twinship by letting them play together so that they could then express their differences as well as similarities. This was indeed an interesting learning point for the research.

There was a deprivation of twin possession, even a grief, like the grief of divorce. The relationship was severed while the wounded individuals survived. There was an unresolved relationship. The outcome, at moments, could look like scrapping, greed, wanting twice as much as was on offer, not wanting to join in but not wanting to be left out, wanting to express four feelings when asked for two, one twin wanting attention when it was being given to the other. I thought about it as a struggle to get enough from a parent, so the need to stock up for twice as long a time as a singleton looks greedy. It was more complicated. To feel full involved ownership of twin as well as parent attachment. As this was forbidden, hunger never got satisfied. Distress was apparent in their expression of "brutality", but it was forbidden to resolve the cause of the distress by owning the opposite sex twin role. The opposite sex twins searched for their twin's attention as much as that of their mother. Every coupling was a triangle.

Brutality, resonance, and marginality are the routes through which opposite sex twin relationship experience can be owned so that the paradox of the social roles can be woven with these private roles. These are further described in Chapter Ten, which describes my journey through the content experience of this research.

The essence of resonance

SEBASTIAN (to Olivia):
So comes it, lady, you have been mistook;
But nature to her bias took in that.
You would have been contracted to a maid;
Nor therein, by my life are you deceiv'd
You are betroth'd both to a maid and a man.

(Shakespeare, *Twelfth Night*, 1601, 5.1: 268–273)

My journey into the cave of opposite sex twins

This chapter draws the many fragments of the archive of the findings in Chapter Nine together, creating a final essence of opposite sex twin experience which illuminates the core of opposite sex twin relationship experience that has emerged from this research.

As I concentrated on the triangular relationship experiences outside of the womb, I seemed to be thrown into the womb, something never discussed by the research group; but, in true psychodramatic style, it pushed its way forward through the labour pains of the physical body, turning into words and giving birth to a place lived in with no words, creating a glorious fanfare of the hidden, forbidden, and preverbal opposite sex twin relationship experience in which preside the essences of *marginality, resonance,* and *brutality.*

I never intended the research to end in the womb. It was meant to illuminate a labyrinth of human relationship activity on earth, to throw energy forward into their future relationship experience, but equally it has pulled me back to the beginning–womb. Having held back from "giving birth" to the essences of this enquiry, I was taken where I did not expect to go. I had started with a template of triangulation: twin, twin, and mother as a primary triangulation and the first building block of opposite sex twin relationship. But, as the research progressed, I was gradually moved towards a dynamic that was in fact more primitive: that the primary relationship was not with mother, but between twins within mother. This was not what I had expected.

In the emergence of this story, it cannot be haphazard that the image of treasure in a cave went straight back to an easily ignored reality that opposite sex twins, like all twins or multiple births, have a relationship for approximately nine months within mother's womb before any other relationship is encountered. This relationship has survived growing and changing, moving and sleeping, touching and banging, sliding and kicking, pressing and pushing, being comfortable as well as uncomfortable in moving waters, suspension, juices, flavours, energies, hormones, each other's emerging bodies. The first and primary relationship with all twins has already been established in the womb through touch, eyes, hearing, body heat, and distance. There are us–me ears and us–me eyes leading to the recognition of an "us" so each twin can find a "me" as well as relating to mother in the early months after birth. All twins have "stolen" nine months of relating from their parents. Perhaps it is earth folk in their singleton world who are denied the opposite sex twins pre-birth experience. It might go some way to explain some of their sexual fantasies, fears, and womb longings. Even ultrasound cannot give more than a pictorial womb experience, but it is not sensorial.

Two of these opposite sex twins were ill and nearly died when very small. This led to further relational confusions of loss and attachment that both the opposite sex twin babies had to navigate and was recently described in a letter from Jim after the research.

What has struck me very powerfully, as a result of the research and other recent experiences, is how strongly embedded are the patterns established in very early childhood and how powerfully they influence our subsequent paths in life.

In my own case, having been born a twin, with no awareness of any other than a twin identity, I was separated from my sister at the age of three months. After a further three months she returned from the nursing home and we were together again throughout our childhood.

The feelings around these events must have begun with a secure feeling of complete identification with my twin followed by a feeling of total aban-donment and intense anguish when she was taken away. These feelings would have been all the stronger because I was helpless, completely unable to care for myself, and also, at the age of three months, unable to give expression to how I felt or understand what was happening. When my sister returned the former pattern was re-established in some measure but I must have felt both dependent on my twin and at the same time unable to completely trust her.

In retrospect, from the perspective of age 64, I can see that my whole life has revolved around this pattern of feelings (security of a twin, separation, anguish, return, mistrust) and indeed that I have, at a subconscious level, choreographed the events of my life to conform in detail with this pattern.

There are two observations I would like to make. The first is that this particular pattern—overlaid onto the common confusions associated with opposite sex twins—has made for a difficult path through life, for me and for the people I have related to. But also, the early experience of separation may have helped me, in a way, to handle the twin dilemma. You will remember from the research that I was the only one of the six twins who saw their twinship as a disadvantage (even a curse) rather than a benign factor and, possibly not coincidentally, I was also the only one of the six who was living with a partner on a permanent basis.

The second observation is that if I had had this insight about childhood patterns earlier in my life I might have been able to respond better to the dilemmas/conundrums I faced and I might have been less trouble to the people I have related to. The fact is that I have searched high and low throughout my adult life—some 40 years—for the knowledge and insight that I needed and had years of counselling, all to little effect. That's why I think your book is important.

These complex brief attachments are no different from any baby in early illness, fostering, or adoption, but it marked up yet another precarious bridge for the psyche of the opposite sex twin to traverse that could lead to difficult relationship experiences not only with parents, but between the twins and with intimate relationships.

The inability to give legitimacy to opposite sex twinship led to difficulties in attachment, ownership, communicating, and consequential misunderstanding. There was stress in the lattice of different essences of meaning; between cultural and fundamental expressions (such as being male but not feeling it); between social and private experience (such as playing with others and denying opposite sex twin connection); and between the psychological and biological (such as opposite sex twins should be different but found so many similarities). These essences kept tripping each other up, so there was no sense of follow through, mirroring the opposite sex twins' experience of being shoved together and pulled apart. Glimpses of playing between opposite sex twins were squashed by the perceived needs of the group, or the internal drama of one, if not each, of the opposite sex twins. When these glimpses of play came there was an ease and tenderness, like babies cooing together, giggling, passing word-sounds back and forth, unquestionably belonging to the moment, absorbed and glued in their spontaneous music making. This was the enviable sensuality of baby play, sticky things to eat, licking fingers, side by side. If this type of play is seen as sexual, it makes all play sexual. If same sex twins play like this it is not seen as sexual. But these opposite sex twins were not encouraged in this glee as they must grow up to find their own partner and soul mate for the continuation of the species. There was little discussion of opposite sex twins loving each other, playing happily, being happy together, or being pleased to be together, and yet this group of opposite sex twins preferred to stay as opposite sex twins even though they were not able to feel pride.

"Love" for each other, a word that was not used in the research, had to be secondary. Brutality and hurt was the closest they got. Love could not be mentioned. It was understood as a dyadic sensation denied these twins after birth. Furthermore, how could love be felt if half of the self, the opposite sex twin self, had to be denied? A failure to be allowed to emerge through the compost of opposite sex twinship led to the uprooting of the opposite sex twin plant from where the seeds fell and the expectation of them to bloom in soil that was not theirs. The twin–self was not loved. It had to change. The glorious experience of feeling sure of your place, being loved and loving, was stolen, because, for opposite sex twins, "love" in the womb was forbidden and love after the womb was hidden. Essentially, opposite sex twins could not separate if twin attachment was not accessible. Single babies started life single; they have to know this sense of singleness in order to reach attachment. This was their primary experience; it was not a twins-in-the womb experience. Twins were never not part of a pair. Therefore, love was a triangle, a panorama.

At base the understanding of the relationship of these opposite sex twins did not appear sexual because their connection was too close, primarily too similar, and in this they were beautiful and before their time. This was not understood about these opposite sex twins. Think of one voice that sings. Think of another voice in duet, find the between, keep it virgin, then you will hear it. Put another way, opposite sex twin relationship is an affair, an illicit affair; not a sexual affair, but an affair of resonance that is beyond male and female. In spite of the opposite sex twins' awareness, this affair exists throughout life. It is irrepressible because it is primitive, a hidden connection laced with the secret, the forbidden, and shame. These opposite sex twins had to hide this resonance at the heart of their being. This led to relationship difficulties as the opposite sex twins searched, possibly unconsciously, for their twin in anyone. The search for their unrequited twin intimacy of resonance could lead to confusion in relationships and in sexual intimacy with adult partners. The ownership of resonance is the route to separation for opposite sex twins. This is at the heart of the cave.

Through all these struggles, this work has led me to the awesome beauty of opposite sex twins, a beauty of resonance depicted in the action and art of the research, which appears to mirror the emerging discoveries in science, psychotherapy, mythology, and, finally, alchemy. All of these illuminate the heart of a cave where can be found a stone of true self through resonance:

> The alchemical brother and sister . . . are united in the chemical wedding in order to produce the philosophers' stone, the perfect platonic union of opposites, upon which the successful outcome of this opus (work) depends . . . [Abraham, 1999, p. 206]

Here, the philosophers' stone refers to an imaginary stone or mineral compound, long sought after by alchemists as a means of transforming other metals into gold. The gold is resonance.

After this long journey of six years, where I thought I had found something new, I could have just looked it up in Abraham's dictionary! But I would not have understood. I do now understand this platonic union where there is a unique balance between similarity and difference between these twins, imperative to the making of peace. Opposite sex twins are not in the same position as same sex twins, because they know and can see there is difference but have not been able to own their similarities. It is through the essences of resonance, brutality, triangulation, marginality, relational distance, and panoramic perception, together with gender roles, that a mobile tapestry is made, illuminating the unique creation of nature, opposite sex twins. The deepest essence is resonance, which shimmers through all other relational experiences and gives them a new perspective, illuminating the relationship experiences of opposite sex twins with unexpected tenderness. As Dan put it:

> *Somebody wrote to me and asked if I would help this bloody woman out with this stupid study that she wants to do, which was really the last thing that I wanted to do. And as we've gone further on listening to everybody else; you know, we have got conflict, we've got harmony, we've got commonality; we have got total differences. I'm delighted to say we are all pretty much on a par in my opinion.*

CHAPTER ELEVEN

The paradox of opposite sex and resonance

> OLIVIA: . . .Alas! It is the baseness of thy fear
> That makes thee strangle thy property.
> Fear not Cesario: take thy fortunes up;
> Be that thou know'st thou art; and then thou art
> As great as that thou fear'st.
>
> (Shakespeare, *Twelfth Night*, 1601, 5.1: 151–155)

Following on from Chapter Ten, I can now see more clearly how difficult it has been to break into talking about opposite sex twins, taboo, gender roles, and hatred, to be able to articulate and illuminate the beauty of nature through opposite sex twins. I, as researcher and opposite sex twin, set out to follow spontaneity and curiosity in understanding the communication of these opposite sex twins through what they did and said and in the gap between them. I have occasionally included my own experience to illustrate a point, through sculpture. It would be interesting for this research to be replicated with another opposite sex twin researcher and opposite sex twin group to see what themes emerged. However, congruent with a psychodrama session, this is what could be offered from this time and place. It is not definitive. We have seen that very small variation in this research can lead to huge changes of attitude so expanding our capacity to curiosity and wonder. It is a small contribution towards illumination of a subject about which there is a need to think and learn. These opposite sex twins exemplify that male and female differences do not prohibit deeper similarities.

There are many opposite sex twins who feel very different from those represented in this book. There are opposite sex twins whose "opposite sex twinship" has been loved, and those who have entirely rejected the phenomena of being an opposite sex twin. There are many parents who have celebrated their opposite sex twins and enjoyed their own important role as their parents. There are parents who brought up their opposite sex twins as if they were not twins at all. There is valuable literature already available for the support of parents, while there is much less for adult opposite sex twins and nothing by adult opposite sex twins. The research has raised challenges to cultural thinking about opposite sex twins in three areas of anxiety:

- fantasy—fantasies of sex in the womb;
- biology—the fear of the emasculation of gender as a threat the species;
- society—the equality of the sexes.

These opposite sex twins have articulated conflict and resonance peculiar to them and, in so doing, have drawn attention to the harmonies and struggles in other human relationships. In these twins there are deep human connections that are often lost to the social roles required for immediate and imperative needs of physical survival. But the focus in this research has been upon the psychic roles of relationship experiences of opposite sex twins that have not been given their rightful place for healthy relationships. Any role that is unresolved psychologically can have a pervasive, even corrosive, effect on other roles. Being able to own the role of opposite sex twin may relieve and liberate the individual self of twin into the hidden dimension of their twinship, so that it can, in turn, contribute to the roles of their individuality and their other relationship experiences.

This chapter sets out to give signposts to carers of twins. These signposts are not pragmatic about the do's and don'ts of twin and family management, as these have been so well provided by others (Appendix 1). This book is about attitude. This attitude observes that very small shifts in conditions can lead to huge changes. For the mind to understand these new arising concepts, it has to be bigger than that subject it is attempting to encompass. It has to be spontaneous.

What does this mean for parents, families, and helpers?

The attitude raised in this research is one of inclusion rather than exclusion. The task for carers is to absorb that the architecture of opposite sex twins means they are conceived and born as an opposite sex pair. This particular ecological architecture is made up of different configurations of the social and cultural expectations that can be in conflict with the primitive internal roles of resonance unique to opposite sex twins and, therefore, to their individuality. It is not only opposite sex twins that have to manage an integration of internal and external roles. But it is the only primitive pre-birth integration that involves male and female roles without, and the male and female duets of resonance within, each twin as well as between them. These opposite sex twins' duets are illustrated by the touching story of an opposite sex twin man who was born some thirty years ago. Three months after his birth, his mother became extremely ill. It was then discovered there was a little girl twin who had died in the womb because they did not know she was there. The opposite sex twin man grew up to dress as a man, and as a woman. In this way, he came to terms with himself as an opposite sex twin and lived his life and the life of his lost twin. He had lived nine months with her in the womb. This is not what every twin must do. It is a metaphor of resolution of self, as opposite sex twin, in order to claim individuality. The earlier the loss of the twin, the more difficult it is to grieve (Hayton, 2007; Woodward, 1998). Opposite sex twins who are deprived of their twin relationship may feel divorced and experience a loss of identity, even while living in the same house as their twin. Some hold that the route to recovery of self is by separation. This research has arrived at a position of separation is by inclusion of opposite sex twinship that is as primal as mothering and "mothering" has rightly been the focus of developmental theory research. So it is hoped that a case has been made for the continuation of research on opposite sex twins in the growing understanding of neurological and psychic significance of relationships in the formation of children's personality and behaviour.

Opposite sex twins challenge their carers' capacity to live, think, and love in threes; to know that when a twin looks at mother they sense their twin, and when they look at their twin they sense 'mother'. Relationships with other members of the family will matter to these twins but will be better enjoyed if the twinship is not excessively envied or excluded by siblings, parents, carers and professional carers. Lewin held that the role of the twin in the psychotherapeutic relationship preceded the role of mother. This sounds as if it is possible for twins to separate these relationships. My position is that the possible role confusion has to be recognized as a natural part of their twin experience before any separation of the roles can emerge. This is in line with the carer's capacity to relate in threes.

Here are the main relational signposts for carers to the understanding of the hum of opposite sex twin duet just out of earshot, that also plays its part in all their other relationships.

The relationship experiences of opposite sex twins

The strengths unique to opposite sex twin men

- They are sensitive, sociable, creative, humorous, and intelligent, and engendering a wish to look after them by their twin sister and others.
- They tend to be special to mother.
- They may see twin–mother as one role.

The vulnerabilities of opposite sex twin men

- They may see fathers preferring their opposite sex twin sister. This is difficult for the men.
- They may lose their twin sister and father who become a pair in his mind.
- They may experience their twin sister as more able and seeing their weaknesses.
- They may feel twin–mother as one role.

The strengths unique to opposite sex twin women

- They are brave, hardworking, diligent, ambitious and caring.

The vulnerabilities of opposite sex twin women

- They are keener on the opposite sex twinship than their opposite sex twin brother.
- They are not sure they are loved by mother and twin.
- They think they earn their relationship with their father.
- They may feel twin–mother as one role.

The strengths of the relationship of these opposite sex twins

- The humming duet of opposite sex twins is always present. It is resonance.
- They feel marginal to their cultural male or female roles.

What they are both vulnerable to

- Fighting between opposite sex twins is not of the same order as same sex twins.
- The envy and dismissal of others may result in their sense of shame, as they do not know how to defend themselves.
- The need for the normalizing of opposite sex twins' experience that can emerge from recognition of the unique qualities of opposite sex twinship that they can internalize as a good enough relationship experience.

Resonance and brutality

Resonance and therefore brutality are embodied. That is to say, they are not thought or felt. They are made manifest in what people do and what happens between them. Resonance is a sympathetic vibration between the opposite sex twins that generates from pre-birth experience. It is the fit in the shared space between the twins. Pleasant or unpleasant, it is earlier and deeper than jealousy, envy, or desire. Resonance is beyond choice. It is harmless. Nothing needs to be done with it except that it does need to be recognized and embraced as part of the individuality of being an opposite sex twin and, as such, a whole human being. Resonance as the phenomenon of opposite sex twins includes a unique balance of male and female between and within each twin that is pivotal to their sense of self. The recognition of this can cause a cascade of relief that, in turn, splashes over guilt and shame of opposite sex twin relationship experiences and illuminates the beauty of resonance. This emerged from the comparison of the paintings and actions of these opposite sex twins.

Brutality is the experience of exclusion by their opposite sex twin that then becomes an internalized exclusion of twin in their psyche. This self-brutalization is an attempt to individuate, because opposite sex twin resonance is seen to dilute the development of the individual position. However, brutality is an inverted sign of resonance that so many other social encounters can overlay or confuse. Paradoxically, the denial of resonance or brutalization in opposite sex twinship does, in fact, dilute the unique individual position of each opposite sex twin. Resonance is the first step on the route to separation, difference, and mental well-being, because resonance is part of the experience of infant omnipotence for opposite sex twins and, therefore, "love", which has been so rarely mentioned.

Intimate relationships

So, for lovers of opposite sex twins, you are not the second, but you do come after. This may make you feel second, and the place to be crowded. The intimacy you have with your opposite sex twin lover may raise unresolved feelings of early attachment that need the seaweed of family relational desires and expectations to be washed off or diluted so that opposite sex twinship can become a good internal experience from which you will benefit. This is not remarkable. Love relationships stir the seaweed in everybody's life, raising unconscious and, therefore, hidden relationships and thereby giving a chance to work them through differently. This discernment is true for all relationships. Parental and sibling relationships are continually renegotiated. Most people have some relationship confusion. Furthermore, choosing an opposite sex twin may have a part to play in your own family experience. It does happen that people keep choosing twins as their partners, so thereby hangs yet another tale.

What your opposite sex twin lover brings to you may be contradictions in their public and private roles; but contradictions or conflicts can belong to everyone. They bring their own peculiar intensity that could be ameliorated by the unique experience of resonance in opposite sex twins. In being allowed to own this, they will enrich and expand their relationship experience with you. You will be a couple of three. It is usual that people bring primary relationships, resolved or unresolved, to their intimate relationships. A couple of three is a common phenomenon. In the development of intimate relationships, all couples have to triangulate so that they do not implode. Opposite sex twins facilitate an opportunity to re-evaluate the male–female roles within each of you and between you. This is a route to the power of gentleness and tenderness.

How would you know if you are meeting an opposite sex twin in a crowd?

Opposite sex twins are not little people. They are full of energy and humour. They are panoramic people. They are likely to be out there contributing to society. They will understand the emotions of those close to them extraordinarily well, but you may feel they do not seem to receive your understanding of them. That might be because they are an opposite sex twin and they might or might not be at ease with it. This was summed up by Kate Maguire in private correspondence. "How I often recognize a twin is the push me pull me dynamic—wanting to be very close, then pulling away into distance almost as if they are ashamed at having exposed themselves to such intimacy so quickly."

Everyone pushes and pulls to some extent. Most people seek a soul mate. But twins, especially opposite sex twins, start life as a pair, possibly a forbidden pair, so they are bound to be seeking their soul mate–twin. They are also bound to relate back to front: intimacy first, distance second. Shame grows at not doing it the other way round, which they gradually learn is generally expected. They are meant to approach a relationship from the outside in, not from the inside out. It is not primitively natural to a twin. It does not mirror their primary attachment experience. Pretending that this is not so does not work. In spite of themselves, twins will twin; so, if it is not with their own twin, it could be anyone. This is not perverse. They did not come into the world alone. They simply magnify what all humans tend to do; search for their best friend. They also mirror a global society of increasing instant, intimate relationships. So, when you meet someone who is easy to relate to or work with, but something in them slips away, there could be many reasons, but one you might not have thought of before is that they might be an opposite sex twin.

As was noted at the start of this book, there may be many content adult opposite sex twins, but there are also opposite sex twins who hate each other, hate being related, hate being hated, and hate being a twin. This hatred is often expressed by living on the other side of the world. It does not work. It leaves holes in their souls, but the landscape of their bodies know.

This research set out to illuminate the relationship experiences of adult opposite sex twins and what they have to teach about the human condition. It centred on learning through the body, and attempts to move towards normalizing an awesome phenomenon, that of opposite sex twins (Figure 12).

Figure 12. Sculpture of opposite sex twins.

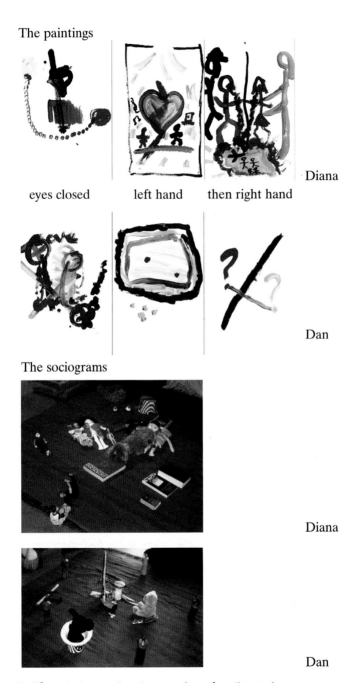

The paintings

Diana

eyes closed   left hand   then right hand

Dan

The sociograms

Diana

Dan

Figure 5. The paintings and sociograms from the pilot study.
(See also the black and white illustration on page 51).

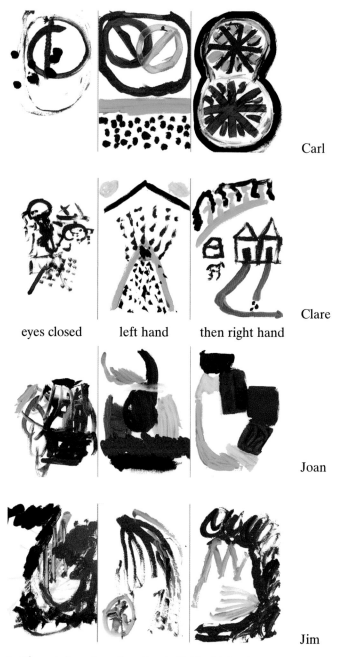

Carl

Clare

eyes closed   left hand   then right hand

Joan

Jim

Figure 6. The paintings from the other individual interviews.
(See also the black and white illustration on page 53).

Carl

Clare

Joan

Jim

Diana

Dan

Figure 9. Their morning paintings (with eyes closed) from Workshop 1. (See also the black and white illustration on page 81).

Carl

Clare

Joan

Jim

Diana

Dan

Figure 10. Their afternoon paintings (with eyes closed) from Workshop 1.
(See also the black and white illustration on page 82).

Organizations for twin care, support, and research

The Multiple Births Foundation (MBF)
Queen Charlotte's & Chelsea Hospital, Level 4
Hammersmith Hospital
Du Cane Road
London W12 OHS
www.multiplebirths.org.uk

Twins and Multiple Births Association (TAMBA)
2 The Willows
Gardener Road
Guildford
GU1 4PG
UK
www.tamba-bsg.org.uk

International Society for Twin Studies (ISTS)
Queensland Institute of Medical Research
Post Office
Royal Brisbane Hospital
Brisbane

Queensland 4029
Australia
www.ists.qimr.edu.au

Center for the Study of Multiple Birth
333 East Superior Street
Suite 464
Chicago
IL 60611
USA
www.multiplebirth.com

Twin Research Unit
St Thomas's Hospital
London, SE1 7EH
www.twin-research

Lone Twin Network
P.O. Box 5653
Birmingham
B29 7JY
UK
Contact by post only.

Wombtwins Survivors
P.O. Box 396
St Albans
Herts
AL3 6NE
UK
www.wombtwin.com

Twinless Twins Support Group International
P.O. Box 980481
Ypsilanti
Missouri 48198-0481
USA
www. Twinlesstwins.org

Multiple Birth Association Bereavement Support Group
P.O. Box 105
Coogee
NSW 2034
Australia
www.amba.org.nz

Twin and Multiple Birth Loss NZ (Inc.)
P. O. Box 51-984,
Pakurange
Auckland
New Zealand
www.twinloss.org.nz

Center for Loss in Multiple Birth (CLIMB), Inc
P.O. Box 91377
Anchorage
Alaska 99509
USA
climb@pobox.alaska.net (Jean Kollantai)

National Organisation of Mothers of Twins Clubs
www.nomotc.org

Glossary

Complementarity: From 'Complementary': two things or more go together making a pair or a whole (*Oxford Compact English Dictionary*, 1996). In the case of twins, complementarity can be reached through the clarification of difference.

Countertransference: The unconscious response to feelings projected onto the self from another, often also a response to transference (see Transference).

Dizygotic twins: These twins are known as fraternal twins and result from the fertilization of two eggs by two spermatozoa. On average these twins share half their genes.

Doubling: Moreno devised this technique as an active form of empathy. The act of doubling represents the developmental stage in infant attachment with the prime figure (mother). Mother contains her new baby to establish the matrix of identity or "This is me" identification in the baby (see Omnipotence). Doubling may also involve some mirroring (see Mirroring).

Irish twins: This is a colloquial term that refers to siblings born less than twelve months apart (Wikipedia).

Locus: A term Moreno employed to describe the presenting scene of distress: e.g., in the present or the recent past.

Mirroring: A technique Moreno devised to facilitate the developmental stage of the child experiencing him/herself as separate from the mother. The child may literally see his/her image in the mirror.

Monozygotic twins: These twins result from the splitting of a single fertilized egg during the first two weeks after conception. These twins share all their genes.

Normosis: A term developed by Moreno to represent the struggle to be normal (see Sharing).

Omnipotence: A psychoanalytic term Melanie Klein used to describe a child's first developmental stage when the world revolves around the self (see Doubling).

Psychodrama: A method developed by Moreno to explore the drama of internal or intra-psychic relationships.

Role reversal: A technique developed by Moreno, and known as the engine of psychodrama. A participant takes the place of another role in his/her story; entering his/her "shoes" to see the world through the eyes of the other role, and experiences the impact of themselves and their own behaviour. Role reversal makes a unique contribution to spontaneity. It represents the child's developmental stage when role-play with others is possible.

Sculpting: A technique used in psychodrama and other action therapies in which people and things can be used to represent internal/external relationships.

Sharing: A term developed by Moreno for group participants to share their identification with themes in the session, discovering that others can feel the same as the self.

Singletons: Children who are not twins; there is only one baby in the womb.

Status nascendi: A term Moreno employed to signify where the scene of distress first arose, usually early in life.

Sociodrama: Moreno developed this method for the exploration of external roles belonging to a group or community: e.g., the role of the policeman, teacher, or parent.

Sociometry: Moreno developed this technique for mapping relationship choices within a group or community to assist the group to find new solutions to problems through "tele" (see Tele).

Spontaneity: This term means a fresh response to an old situation, or an adequate response to a new situation. Moreno saw spontaneity as life force or "act hunger" that was often inhibited by what he called "cultural conserve", or the culture restrictions to spontaneity.

Transference: This is generally understood as the passing on, displacing, or "transferring" of an emotion or affective attitude from one person to another person or object. Within psychoanalysis and other psychotherapies, feelings and attitudes towards other persons (usually one's parents, but also siblings or spouse, etc) are projected into and often re-enacted in the relationship with the therapist. This projected relationship is often infantile. "The analyst is nudged into living . . . the transference relationship with the patient and is then able to recognise and interpret it" (Lewin, 2004, p. 119). Transference can be described as positive or negative, depending on whether the feelings towards the analyst in this context are pleasant or hostile. Transference can be regarded as a normal component in human interaction, but in a therapy situation the neutrality of the practitioner creates the conditions for it to be more clearly observable.

Moreno described transference as: "The pathological portion of the universal factor [called the], Tele" (Moreno, 1934, p. 56).

Tele: A term developed by Moreno to describe the unconscious attractions, repulsion, or indifference towards others. Tele is intrinsic to spontaneity and central to the technique of sociometry (see Sociometry).

Warming up: Moreno recognized that spontaneity was not constant and therefore had to be prepared for through bringing focus to the present moment.

Zygote: A fertilized egg that will develop into an embryo, and eventually into a mature organism.

REFERENCES

Abraham, H. (1953). Twin relationship and womb fantasies in a case of anxiety hysteria. *International Journal of Psychoanalysis, 34*: 219–27.

Abraham, L. (1999). *The Dictionary of Alchemical Imagery*. Cambridge: Cambridge University Press.

Abrams, S., & Neubauer, P. (1994). Hartmann's vision. *Psychoanalytic Study of the Child, 49*: 49–59.

Anzieu, D. (1979). The sound image of the self. *International Review of Psycho-Analysis, 6*: 23–36.

Aries, P. (1962). *Centuries of Childhood. A Social History of Family Life*. New York: Vintage.

Athanassiou, C. (1986). A study in the vicissitudes of identification in twins. *International Journal of Psychoanalysis, 67*: 329–336.

Bainham, A., Day Sclater, S., Richards, M., & Cambridge Socio-Legal Group (1999). *What is a Parent? A Socio-legal Analysis*. Oxford: Hart.

Barth, J. (1960). *The Sotweed Factor. Lost in the Fun House*. London: Atlantic.

Bertolucci, B. (2003). *The Dreamers*. Film.

Bettelheim, B. (1969). *The Children of the Dream*. London: Macmillan.

Bick, E. (1968). The experience of the skin in early object relations. *International Journal of Psychoanalysis, 49*: 484–486.

Bick, E. (1986). Further considerations on the function of the skin in early objects relations. *British Journal of Psychotherapy, 2*: 292–413.

Bion, W. R. (1967). The imaginary twin. In: *Second Thoughts. Selected Papers in Psychoanalysis* (pp. 3–22). New York: Jason Aronson.

Bion, W. R., & Foulkes, S. H. (1985). Basic assumptions and beyond. In: M. Pines (Ed.), *Bion and Group Psychotherapy*. London: Jessica Kingsley.

Blatner, A., & Blatner, A. (1988). *Foundations of Psychodrama, History, Theory & Practice*. New York: Springer.

Boadella, D. (2001). Morphodynamics, neuroscience and psycho-energetics: the roots of biosynthesis as a form of somatic psychotherapy. Paper presented to the Seventh Professional Conference of the UK Council for Psychotherapy, "Revolutionary Connections: Psychotherapy and Neuroscience".

Boklage, C. E. (1985). Interactions between opposite-sex-dizygotic fetuses and the assumptions of the Weinberg difference method epidemiology. *American Journal of Human Genetics, 37*: pp. 591–605.

Boklage, C. E. (2005). *Embryogenesis of Chimeras, Twins and Anterior Midline Asymmetries. Human Reproduction*. Oxford University Press, on behalf of the European Society of Human Reproduction and Embryology, on line October 2005.

Bowlby, J. (1988). *A Secure Base. Clinical Applications of Attachment Theory*. London: Routledge.

Braud, W., & Anderson, R. (1998). *Transpersonal Research Methods for the Social Sciences*. London: Sage.

Bry, L. (1999). Can identical twins be opposite genders? MadSci Network: General Biology [internet]. Available from: www.madsci.org/posts/archives/jul99/931746434.Gb.r.html (posted 11 July 1999).

Bryan, E. M. (1983). *The Nature & Nurture of Twins*. London: Bailliere Tyndall.

Burlingham, D. T. (1952). *Twins. A Study of Three Pairs of Identical Twins*. London: Imago.

Byng-Hall, J. (1995). *Rewriting Family Scripts*. New York: Guilford Press.

Casson, J. (1998). www.communicube.co.uk

Coles, P. (2002). The children in the apple tree: some thoughts on sibling attachment. In: B. Bishop, et al. (Eds.), *Practice of Psychotherapy Series: Book 2*. London: Karnac.

Coles, P. (2003). *The Importance of Sibling Relationships in Psychoanalysis*. London: Karnac.

Cole-Harding, S., Morstad, A. L., & Wilson, J. R. (1988). Spatial ability in members of the opposite sex twin pairs. *Behaviour Genetics, 18*: 710.

Cozolino, L. (2002). *The Neuroscience of Psychotherapy*. London: Norton.

Dalal, F. (1998). *Taking the Group Seriously*. London: Jessica Kingsley.

Davis, D. L., & Davis, D. (2004a). Acting the part: identity politics and the performance of twinship at twin festivals in the USA. Paper presented to the 11th ICTS Conference, Denmark.

Davis, D. L., & Davis, D. I. (2004b). I–WE, ME–YOU, US–THEM: navigating hyphens of intersubjctivity among sets of identical twins. Paper presented to the Annual Meeting of the European Association of Social Anthropologists. Session on "Between identity and alterity: engaging in shared experience of everyday life". Vienna, Austria, September.

Davison, S. (1992). Mother, other and self-love and rivalry for twins in their first year of life. *International Review of Psychoanalysis, 19*: 359–374.

Descartes, R. (1637). *Discourse on Method*, J. Veitch (Trans). New York: Dutton, 1988.

Descartes, R. (1977). *The Essential Writings*, J. J. Bloom (Trans.) New York: Harper & Row.

Dibble, E., & Cohen, D. (1981). Personality development in identical twins—the first decade of life. *Psychoanalytic Study of the Child, 36*, 45–70.

Dunbar, R. (1996). *Gossip, Grooming and the Evolution of Language*. Cambridge, MA: Harvard University Press.

Engel, G. (1975). The death of a twin: mourning and anniversary reactions. Fragments of 10 years' analysis. *International Journal of Psychoanalysis, 56*: 23–40.

Eysenck, H. G., & Wilson, G. (1979). *The Psychology of Sex*. London: Dent & Sons.

Fischbein, D. (1978). School achievement and test results for twins and singletons in relation to social background. In: P. Magnus, K. Berg & W. E. Nance (Eds.), *Twin Research: Part A. Psychology and Methodology*. New York: Liss.

Fischbein, D., Ove, F., & Cenner, S. (1991). Popularity ratings of twins & non twins at age 11 and 13. *Scandanavian Journal of Educational Research, 35*: 227–238.

Fox, J. (Ed.) (1987). *The Essential Moreno*. New York: Springer.

Freud, S. (1900a). *The Interpretation of Dreams*. S.E., 4–5, pp. 339–626. London: Hogarth.

Freud, S. (1912–1913). *Totem and Taboo*. S.E., 13: 1–162. London: Hogarth.

Freud, S. (1923). The ego and the super ego. In: *The Ego and the Id and other Works. S.E., 19*: 28–39.

Gibran, K. (1992). *The Prophet*. London: Penguin.

Glenn, J. (1966). Opposite sex twins. *Journal of the American Psychoanalytic Association, 14*: 736–759.

Hartmann, H. (1952). A review of *Twins*, by D. Burlingham. *Psychoanalytic Study of the Child, 36*: 147–150.

Hayton, A. (2007). *Untwinned*. St Albans: Wren.

Hegel, G. W. F. (1807). *Phenomenology of Spirit*, A. V. Miller & J. N. Findlay (Trans.). New York: Oxford University Press, 1979.

Heidegger, M. (1977). *Basic Writings*, D. Krell (Ed.). New York: Harper & Row.

Holmes, P. (1992). *The Inner World Outside*. London: Routledge.

Hume, D. (1751). *An Enquiry Concerning Human Understanding*. Oxford: Oxford University Press, 1999.

Hume, D. (1777). *Enquiry Concerning Human Understanding and the Principle of Morals* (3rd edn). Oxford: Clarendon Press, 1975.

Husen, T. (1959). *Psychological Twin Research*. Stockholm: Almqvist & Wiksell.

Husserl, E. (1931). *Ideas*. W. R. Boyce Gibson (Trans.). London: George Allen & Unwin.

Husserl, E. (1970). *Logical Investigations*, Volume 1. J. N. Findlay (Trans). New York: Humanities.

James, O. (2007). *Affluenza*. London. Vermilion.

Jennings, S. (1992). *Dramatherapy with Families, Groups and Individuals*. London: Jessica Kingsley.

Kant, I. (1781). *Critique of Pure Reason*, N. Kemp Smith (Trans.). London: Palgrave Macmillan, 1926.

Kenneth, D., Kochanek, M. A., Joyce, A., & Martin, M.P.H. (2008). U.S. Department of Health and Human Services in the National Center for Health Statistics. Available at: www.cdc.gov/nchs/products/pubs/pubd/hestats/infantmort/infantmort.htm (last reviewed October 2008).

Kipper, D. A. (1986). *Psychotherapy through Role-playing*. New York: Brunner/Mazel.

Klaning, U., Bo Mortensen, P., & Ohm Kyvik, K. (1996). Increased occurrence of schizophrenia and other psychiatric illnesses amongst twins. *The British Journal of Psychiatry, 168*: 668–692.

Klein, M. (1932). *The Psycho-Analysis of Children*. London: Hogarth, 1980.

Klein, M. (1963). On the sense of loneliness. In: *Envy and Gratitude and Other Works* (pp. 300–313). London: Hogarth, 1980.

Klein, M. (1986). In: J. Mitchell (Ed.), *The Selected Melanie Klein*. London: Penguin.

Koch, H. L. (1955). Some personality correlates of sex, sibling position and sex of sibling among five and six year old children. *Genetic Psychology Monographs*, 52: 3–50.

Koch, H. L. (1966). *Twins and Twin Relations*. Chicago, IL: University of Chicago Press.

Kohut, H. (1971). *The Analysis of the Self—A Systematic Approach to the Psychoanalytic Treatment of Narcissistic Personality Disorders*. New York: International University Press.

Kruger, R. F. (2001). Current directions in personality research with twins. Paper presented at the ICTS Conference, London.

Lacan, J. (1993). *The Seminar of Jacques Lacan: Book III, The Psychoses (1955–1956)*, J. A. Miller (Ed.). London: Norton.

Lacombe, P. (1959). The problem of the identical twin as reflected in a masochistic compulsion to cheat. *International Journal of Psychoanalysis*, 40: 6–12.

Laffey-Ardley, S., & Thorpe, K. (2006). Being opposite: is there advantage of being an opposite-sex twin? *Journal of the International Society for Twin Studies*, 9(1): 131–140.

Lewin, V. (1994). Working with a twin: implications for the transference. *British Journal of Psychotherapy*, 10: 499–510.

Lewin, V. (2004). *Twins in the Transference*. London: Whurr.

Linton, R. (1936). *The Study of Man*. New York: Appleton Century.

Luzes, P. (1990). Fact and fantasy in brother–sister incest. *International Review of Psychoanalysis*, 17: 97–113.

Maenchen, A. (1968). Object cathexis in a borderline twin. *Psychoanalytic Study of the Child*, 23: 438–456.

Marsdon, P. (2001). Double blind. Anorexia nervosa in monozygotic twins. Paper presented at the ICTS Conference, London.

McDonald, A. (2001). One and one make three: a grounded theory study of twinship and the needs of twins in psychological counselling. Paper presented to the Congress for the International Congress for the Society of Twin Studies, ICTS. Unpublished.

McFadden, D. (1993). A masculinizing effect on the auditory systems of the human females having male co-twins. *Proceedings of the National Academy of Sciences USA*, 90: 11900–11904.

Mead, G. H. (1934). *Mind, Self and Society*. Chicago, IL: University of Chicago Press.

Mead, R. (1704). On the influence of the sun and moon upon human bodies and the diseases arising there from. *Wikipedia*, accessed August 2008.

Meltzer, D. (1975). Adhesive identification. *Contemporary Psychoanalysis, 11*: 289–310.

Miller, E. M. (1994). Stalking the wild taboo. Prenatal sex hormone transfer: a reason to study opposite sex twins. *Personality and Individual Differences, 17*(4): 511–529.

Mitchel, J. E., Baker, L. A., & Jacklin, C. N. (1989). Masculinity and femininity in twin children: genetic and environmental factors. *Child Development, 60*: 1475–1485.

Mitchell, J. (2000). *Mad Men and Medusas. Reclaiming Hysteria and The Effect of Sibling Relationships on the Human Condition*. London: Penguin.

Mitchell, J. (2003). *Siblings*. Cambridge: Polity Press.

Montessori, M. (1963). *The Absorbent Mind*. Madras: Vasanta Press.

Moreno, J. L. (1934/1953). *Who Shall Survive?* Beacon, NY: Beacon House [reprinted 1953]; American Society of Group Psychotherapy & Psychodrama (Eds.). Virginia: Royal Publishing Company [reprinted 1993].

Moreno, J. L. (1941). *The Words of the Father*. New York: Beacon House.

Moreno, J. L. (1946). *Psychodrama*. Volume I (3rd edn). New York: Beacon House.

Moreno, J. L., & Moreno, F. B. (1994). *Spontaneity Theory of Child Development*. Psychodrama Monographs, 8. New York: Beacon House.

Moustakas, C. (1994). *Phenomenological Research Methods*. London: Sage.

Ortmeyer, D. (1970). The weself of identical twins. *Contemporary Psychoanalysis, 6*: 125–142.

Parens, H. (1988). Siblings in early childhood: some direct observational findings. *Psychoanalytic Inquiry, 8*: 31–50.

Penninkilampi-Kerola,V., Kaprio, J., Moilanen, I., Ebeling, H., & Rose, R. J. (2004). Co-twin dependence and twins' psycho-emotional wellbeing & health from adolescence to early adulthood. A longitudinal study of development and health of five consecutive birth cohorts of Finnish twins. Paper presented at the ICTS Conference, Denmark.

Pierce, C. S. (1934). *Collected Papers of Charles Sanders Pierce*. C. Harshorne & P. Weiss (Eds.). Cambridge, MA: Harvard University Press.

Piontelli, A. (2002). *Twins, From Foetus to Child*. London: Routledge.

Proner, K. (2000). Protomental synchrony; some thoughts on the earliest identification processes in a neonate. *International Journal of Infant Observation, 3:* 55–63.

Record, R. G., McKeown T., & Edwards, J. H. (1970). An investigation of the difference in measured intelligence between twins and single births. *Annals of Human Genetics, 34:* 11–20.

Reil, J. C. (1957). In: E. Harms, Modern psychotherapy – 150 years ago. *Journal of Mental Science, 103:* 804–809.

Resnick, S. M., Gottesman, I. L., & McGue, M. (1993). Sensation seeking in opposite-sex twins: an effect of prenatal hormones? *Behaviour Genetics, 23:* 323–332.

Rosambeau, M. (1987). *How Twins Grow Up*. London: Bodley Head, 1999.

Rosenfeld, H. (1971). Contribution to psychopathology of psychotic states: the importance of projective identification in the ego structure and the object relations of the psychotic patient's problems in psychosis. *Exerpta Medica*, 115–128. [Reprinted in: E. Bott Spillius (Ed.), *Melanie Klein Today. Developments in Theory and Practice, Vol. 1: Mainly Theory* (pp. 117–137). London: The New Library of Psycho-analysis 7, in association with the Institute of Psycho-Analysis, 1988.]

Roy, A. (1997). *The God of Small Things*. London: Harper Perennial.

Sandbank, A. (1988). *Twins and the Family*. London: Arrow, 2003.

Sandbank, A. (Ed.) (1999). *Twin and Triplet Psychology*. London: Routledge.

Schore, A. N. (1996). The experience dependent maturation of a regulatory system in the orbital prefrontal cortex and the origin of developmental psychopathology. *Development and Psychopathology, 8:* 59–87.

Schore, A. N. (2001). Minds in the making: attachment, the self-organising brain and developmentally orientated psychoanalytic psychotherapy. *British Journal of Psychotherapy, 17:* pp. 299–328.

Schutzenberger, A. A. (1998). *The Ancestor Syndrome*. London: Routledge.

Segal, N. L. (1999). *Entwined Lives*. New York: Dutton.

Segal, N. L. (2009). Personal correspondence.

Segal, N. L., Hersberger, N. L., & Arad, S. (2003). Meeting one's twin: perceived social closeness and familiarity. *Evolutionary Psychology, 1:* 70–95.

Shakespeare, W. (1601). *Twelfth Night, or As You Like It*. W. J. Craig (Ed.), London: Oxford University Press, 1957.

Sheerin, D. F. (1991). Fundamental considerations in the psychotherapy of an identical twin. *British Journal of Psychotherapy, 8*(1): 13–25.

Siemon, M. (1980). The separation/individuation process in adult twins. *American Journal of Psychotherapy, 34*(3): 387–400.

Smith, J. D. (1988). *Psychological Profiles of Con-joint Twins: Hereditary, Environment and Identity.* Connecticut & London: Praeger.

Steiner, J. (1993). *Psychic Retreats. Pathological Organisations in Psychotic, Neurotic and Borderline Patients.* London: Routledge.

Stern, D. N. (1985). *The Interpersonal World of the Infant. A View from Psycho-analysis and Developmental Psychology.* New York: Basic Books.

Stern, D. N., Bruschweiler-Stern, N., & Freeland, A. (1998). *The Birth of a Mother.* London: Bloomsbury.

Stocks, P., & Karns, M. N. (1933). A biometric investigation of twins and their brothers and sisters, Pt. II. *Annals of Eugenics, 5*: 1–55.

Stuart, E. (2001). *Exploring Twins: Towards a Social Analysis of Twinship.* New York: Palgrave Macmillan.

Swanson, P. B. (2001). When is a twin not a twin? Paper presented to the 10th ICTS Conference, London.

Tambyraja, R. L., & Ratnam, S. S. (1981). Plasma steroid changes in twin pregnancies. In: L. Gedda, P. Parisi, & W. E. Nance (Eds.), *Twin Research 1; Part A. Twin Biology and Multiple Pregnancy* (pp. 190–195). Netherlands: Springer.

Taubman-Ben-Ari, O., Findler, L., & Kuint, L. (2004). Mental health as a function of internal and external resources among mothers of twins and singletons. Poster presentation at the 11th ICTS Conference, Denmark.

Thorpe, K., & Gardner, K. (2006). Twins and their twinships: differences between monozygotic, dizygotic same-sex and dizygotic mixed-sex pairs. *Journal of the International Society for Twin Studies, 9*(1): 155–165.

Trapp, R. (1986). The role of disagreement in interactional argument. *Journal of the American Association, 23*(1): 23–41.

Trevarthen, C. (2003). Neuroscience and intrinsic psychodynamics: current knowledge and potential for therapy. In: J. Corrigall & H. Wilkinson (Eds.), *Revolutionary Connections.* London: Karnac.

Vinterberg, T. (1999). *Festen.* Film.

Wagner, R. (1870). *The Ring Cycle: The Valkyrie* (opera).

Watt, D. (2003). Psychotherapy in the age of neuroscience. New opportunities in the renaissance of affective neuroscience. In: J. Corrigal & H. Wilkinson (Eds.), *Revolutionary Connections.* London: Karnac.

Wilder, T. (1927). *The Bridge of San Luis Rey*. London: Harper Perennial, 2003.

Williams, A. (1991). *Forbidden Agendas*. London: Routledge.

Winnicott, D. (1990). Ego distortion in terms of true and false self. In: *The Maturational Processes and the Facilitating Environment*. London: Karnac.

Wisot, A. (2008). With Reproductive Partners Medical, Redondo Beach, California, in babyrazzi.com, 24 July.

Woodward, J. (1998). *The Lone Twin*. London: Free Association.

Zazzo, R. (1960). *Les Jumeaux, le couple et la person*. Paris: Presses Universitaires.

Zazzo, R. (1976). The twin condition and the couple effects on personality development. *Acta Geneticae Medicae et Gemellologiae, 25*: 243–352.

INDEX